The

Greatful Dad

A CEO's Best Friend

A Teacher's Best Friend

A Wife's Best Friend

A Child's Best Friend

John R. Trayser

Front cover photo by Austin James Trayser
Back cover photo Holly Potts, photographer, Bozeman, MT

This book was edited with love by Ms. Savannah Barnes of Montana State University, Bozeman, Montana

ISBN 13: 978-0-9791098-0-5
ISBN 10: 0-9791098-0-9
Printed in the United States of America

Contents

Dedication

This book is dedicated to Grace and Vernon Trayser, my two incredibly gifted parents. They gave their love each day unconditionally in every direction they looked. Their influence on their children and friends remains a legacy that will be felt for generations to come.

I was in Montana the day my mother died and I could feel the freedom of her spirit being released from her earthly body. I know she looks down on us from heaven hoping that her kindness leaves a trail of goodness for her family. Rest assured mother dear that your spirit has been passed on to my boys. They didn't have the chance to know you as I did, but people who meet them also know you...

I was lucky enough to be notified that my father's breathing was becoming very labored and had the opportunity to say a personal good bye to the man I owed my life to. As I held his hand at the very moment of his passing all I could do was repeat, "thank you dad." For each moment of caring, giving and support that he gave without measure, I feel blessed to have been placed in such an incredibly loving environment.

I simply feel compelled to share the love that they gave so freely to every person they met. Invest a few hours in learning how they laid a path for us to walk on each day. There wasn't five minutes of my life where I didn't feel safe, can you say the same?

Introduction

I want to change the world, brick by brick. It's that simple. I have seen in my fifty six years way too many unhappy adult children. I believe I know where they come from. I want to herald the end of the Dysfunctional Family.

My simple philosophy is this: When you have your first child, and go to the hospital to get Mom and the baby, an amazing thing happens in the parking lot. God or the stork sneaks a load of bricks into the trunk of your car. From the moment you arrive at home you have two choices of what to do with those bricks. You can either build a path for your child to safely walk on, or you can build a wall between you and your child....

Stop right there! Did you feel that? You already know how the bricks were used at your house, didn't you? What I have discovered is this. Every relationship works exactly the same. Every word, motion, look or touch either builds a path or a wall.

The infamous Dysfunctional Family comes from using those bricks to build walls on a regular basis. As a result of those walls being built, two very crippling emotions are established in a child's formative years that may haunt them for the rest of their lives. Fear and doubt are the two most tragic and painful emotions a human can have. They are the emotions that keep self esteem from growing. If not checked in the early years before school is started, the result is a cracked mirror reflection that inhibits the use of those bricks to be used as the mortar in the relationship building process for the rest of your life.

This book was written as a result of two very simple events. First, when my middle son was a third grader, my wife and I were asked to come in very early for a school parent/teacher conference. My son was also in attendance. The teacher said that she had asked us to come in first so that she could hold on to the feeling that comes from a child actually learning and contributing to her class as a result of her daily effort. My wife was also a teacher and nodded in the agreement of that statement. She said that 90 % of the parents coming in for conferences ask why they are not doing more for their child at school. Instead she thanked me for all the times I had come in to read to the class, gone on field trips or attended a party.

The teacher looked at my son and then looked at us and said these amazing words, "Your son has shown me something that I have not seen in twenty two years of teaching. He watches over the entire class with a spirit that says, shouldn't we all be watching over each other?" My wife looked at the teacher and replied as she looked over at me and said, "Well, you just made his life complete."

She was absolutely correct! I was immediately wondering whether Dairy Queen was open at 8:00 am so that we could celebrate! She added that she had questioned my youngest son's first grade teacher and found that he carried the same spirit with him in her class as well. She then said these simple words to me, "If you could ever put in writing what you have done to make them look at the world this way, it would be the teacher's greatest friend."

I grabbed my son out of his chair and gave him the biggest hug he maybe had ever had! We were so busy celebrating as we left the school that I didn't really grasp the significance of what she had said to me. It took one more event a few weeks later that rekindled that meeting's importance.

I was in Nashville, Tennessee for a weekend of music and friendship with my long time buddy Dickie Brown. He had a group of musician friends over to his home on an informal basis every once in a while and was kind enough to invite me to slide down from Chicago for a few days of revelry.

As the night was wearing down, a handful of ladies were sequestered in front of the fireplace talking about their childhoods. One woman said this simple statement. "I don't think my parents hated us, I just don't think they knew what to do with us." It was like a lightning bolt had hit me square between the eyes! I wanted to jump up and scream that I knew exactly what to do with children! That's what the teacher had told me! I knew what to do with the bricks that my parents had laid in front of me every day to walk on safely. There wasn't one five minute period in my childhood where I had any doubt or fear of how my parents felt about me. Never!

That is what this book is about. The things you can do to make your children feel safe every day. It starts the day they are born and it never ends. The amazing thing is that there is a circle of behavior that is established that allows you to use these same principles in every facet of your life. You are building walls or paths every day with the words or actions you use in your daily life.

There is a license for driving a car, for using a boat, even for having a dog some times. Yet, there is no requirement for how to care for your child. My goal is to change the world one brick at a time. If you feel that your life should have been different and that you are curious as to how you can make changes, you are in the right place. If you think that it is too late to make a difference in the lives of your children, you are absolutely WRONG!

It is never too late to show someone you care. What you need to accept as truth is this; we are all just children from the time we are born to the day we die. We just get older. We all have the same desire to be loved, the desire to belong and most importantly, to be appreciated and cared for being just who we are.

That is our mission as parents. To lay down that path for our children to walk safely on and in every way possible help those in our own families and others in our daily lives see a reflection in our eyes that make them feel valued for just who they are. That is what my children have taught me. Nothing in life is more important than that. Leaving a legacy of happy children is the greatest gift you can leave the world. Of that I am absolutely certain!

As an important footnote; this book was originally written and self published ten years ago in that initial burst of enthusiasm. My three sons are now 27, 20 and 18 years of age. My confidence levels in the ideas I share in this book are deeply entrenched. My children continue to watch over others on a daily basis and make me look good quite often. HOWEVER, they are not angels. I will try to link the lessons they were taught as children to the behaviors I see them having as young adults. They often make me feel like the most Grateful Dad in the world....

Chapter One

Brick by Brick

The Path

*I*f you take only one concept away from this book, let it be this one. I discovered that in my lifetime that every word, look, emotion or touch has an impact far greater than we understand. The impact we make on others is predicated by the actions and words we impart on others.

Remember this, I believe that the tools we are given for building relationships with our children are EXACTLY the same ones that we use in our daily lives to develop relationships with friends, clients and strangers.

I also believe that success in raising our children and establishing strong relationships with friends and business associates are based on the removal of fear and doubt. Here is the first brick for you to try. If you feel the power of this one you may be more likely to try the next one, which is what my goal is.

Okay, here goes: regardless of your relationship with your child, or even the age of the child, take your two hands and place them on both sides of their face. Now look them right in the eyes and say these MAGIC words. THERE IS NOTHING I WOULDN'T DO FOR YOU!

I'm serious about this. If you make the effort and do it with sincerity, you will find the power of this action unbelievably strong. I know you have made your best effort to connect with your child since the day he/she was born. However, the simple act of making so clear a statement does one very amazing thing. It eliminates any doubt that your child may have. It works on the very young and it works in every relationship you have.

I believe that it is a two way exchange that has all the power in the world! I am fairly certain it is the key factor in all my success in my business life as well. Once you understand the power of the statement, it becomes the way you deal with everyone. **It is the source of unconditional love.** Wow! I just now discovered the impact of that statement. That is why people respond to me the way they do. My positive attitude seems to affect people on a regular basis. It is what my children have picked up over the years. The SINCERITY of this attitude is what allows them to find the strength to watch over other people. That is what the teacher was telling us about that so amazed her at that fateful third grade conference. (See introduction)

If you find the courage to try that statement, I promise you something will change in your head. You will find that the feeling you get and give is everything you needed and wanted from your family. I have found that LOVE BY ASSUMPTION is love that contains doubt.

I remember very clearly asking my wife during a late night, emotional conversation if she thought her parents would "do anything" for her. She sat for a couple of minutes, which seemed like hours, and finally said, "I think they might have." I slowly nodded my head and asked what had taken so long to decide. She said, "Because they never said anything like that."

I slowly smiled. At that moment, a very bright halogen light went off in her head. She looked right at me and said, "Is that what you have been waiting for me to say all of these years?" Tears at that point were rolling down my face. You see, I had been telling her for years that there was nothing I wouldn't do for her. I was doing the same thing for my children, but frankly I had doubt about the depth of my wife's love for me for one simple reason. She had never gone over the wall that her folks had built around her as a little girl. We had been married for twenty years at this point in time. I guess I was DYING to hear those words from her. I did have doubt about how she cared for me. She was brought up by the love by assumption concept. I believe it still affects her daily life still today.

I know that may sound a little too simple, yet that is the secret to a strong relationship/friendship. Having the other person believe that there is nothing you wouldn't do for them is the mortar that holds all the bricks together. It is what makes a marriage last. It is the mortar that makes a business relationship last when a mistake is made or times get tough in any way. I remember saying clearly to my clients that no matter what, I would be there for them. If operations or administration were to make a mistake, I promised I would not hide from it, but would make sure that things were fixed as soon as possible. The amazing thing is, you can actually **score some points** with a client/child/friend by backing up your words by standing by them when times get tough. Sounds like that unconditional love thing again!

Please make an effort to try this first brick. I remember having a great conversation a few years ago with an old business associate to whom I had sent a copy of my self-published book. Jenny had always been like a sponge as our business relationship grew. I had plucked her out of the operations department to work with me as my sales associate. Her outgoing manner made her an ideal candidate for supporting my efforts in field. I couldn't have been more right about that.

Years after we had worked together, we were still great phone friends. Every so often we would connect on the phone to hear what was going on in each others lives. I have developed a policy of when I think of someone, I make the effort to pick up the phone and give them a call. You only have to say one thing, "I was just thinking about you." Almost always people would say, "I thought about you the other day." I was happy that they thought about me, but was sad that it was not important enough for them to pick up the phone. Life is so short…

Well, I digress. Jenny called me a week or so later, all excited, after I had sent her the book. She said she had devoured the book in one sitting. Most people had the same reaction. It was short and formatted in a way that was conducive to immediate consumption. She wanted to share her reaction to one very specific part of the book. She had been captivated by the 'There's nothing I wouldn't do for you" statement. For some reason it struck a responsive chord her in head and heart. She thought she might give it a try with her young children. She told me that she had felt that way about them from birth, as most of us do, but the significance of the physical act seemed to be very important as she thought about it.

She said she hoped that it would make an impression on them and potentially remove any doubt that they might have about her love as their mother. So she gave it a try. The reason she called me was to tell me that she was so grateful for the idea. Her BIG surprise was the effect that it had on her. She was physically and emotionally shaking a bit at the end of the experience. Here is why. As we get so busy being parents, the physical side of taking care of our children becomes the obvious point of reference because there is so much to do. Feeding, diapers, clothing, bathing, shopping and driving are the lifeblood of the early year's effort. Add a second or third child and whammo! you are overwhelmed with the level of responsibility that comes with parenting.

I mean overwhelmed! If you have been at home through this process, then you know what I mean. Well, Jenny stopped the train of physical caring for just that moment and took her shot at the hands on the face thing. At first, the child didn't really acknowledge the sincerity of the moment. So she tried it again with her gently pulling the face back to her, so that their eyes met in a solid connection. She said, "No, you don't understand yet. There is absolutely nothing I wouldn't do for you." I don't remember how old her child was, and that is not the point of the story really. What was really important was the connection for Jenny first. She had made clear to the child that there was no room for doubt in their relationship. The mortar had been mixed and applied two times that day so that if tomorrow things got out of control, as life often does, the child would have heard a clear statement of unconditional love. It so impacted Jenny that she needed to call and share the moment with me. That alone says something about the power of that statement.

I am now fifty six years old. I remember the times my mother did this for me as if it were yesterday. Again, I believe this physical/emotional effort is the foundation belief that is the mortar that makes all the difference in the world as your children are growing up. Without doubt, there is room for self esteem to grow. With doubt, you may have the beginnings of a wall growing between you, that you may find harder to climb over, through or around as time goes on. Every day you have to decide if you are building a path or a wall. It never changes. And more importantly, it is never too late to break down a wall or choose to build a path instead. We all crave the acceptance of our parents, right?

The Wall

Unconditional love is the first brick in building a path for our children to walk on safely. Now it is time to explore what a brick looks like that builds a wall between a child and a parent. I believe I have found the one statement that creates more unhappiness, confusion, resentment and frustration in the lives of children and therefore adults, than any one other statement. Here it is: **Why can't you be more like.....?**

Fill in any name or idea at the end of the sentence. Here is the first ingredient in a recipe for disaster. This brick is a hard one to overcome or destroy once it has been laid at the foundation of the wall. In a family of more than one child, there is a natural comparison of one child to another sibling. However, our goal as parents should be to find wonder, amazement and joy in the differences between the siblings, not to constantly measure one's behavior against the other. The most amazing thing my parents accomplished with our family was this. Each one of us, I know, thought we were the favorite child.

Let me give you a real life example with this short story. I invited my mother to downtown Chicago, to a very nice restaurant, to tell her as best I could what her love and support had meant to me growing up. I was about thirty years old and my business career was starting to take off. I was the "rising superstar" of the Trust Department of a major bank. I felt that my parent's effort had paid off handily and gave them most of the credit for my success. I had been noticing the way I was different from other sales people in my financial services world.

We never had a great deal of money and my mom had started selling real estate to supplement the income required to send four boys to college. Romantic that I am, I purchased a gold necklace for my mom to wear as a reminder of what her love had meant to one of her boys. There were tears and hugs right there in the restaurant as I told her what her effort had meant to me. It was a super warm fuzzy moment for a son and his mother. In the car, on the way to taking her to the train, to head back home, for some reason, I said these words, "You don't have to say anything mom, but I know I am your favorite." Without a moments hesitation and a quick glance at me she responded, "That's funny because your brother Dave said that same thing to me about three weeks ago."

Oh come on!!!!!! There is no way he would have said that. He is not the demonstrative one in the family! He is the quiet one and does not share his feelings easily or wear his heart on his sleeve like me! No way he could have said that! Until this day, I still have my doubts. Yet, she said it with such a great poker face that it took the wind right out of my sails. It didn't diminish the value or heart of the day, but it taught me the magic of making sure that each child is loved in their own unique way.

I have seen up close through friends of my children and people I have know how painful it is to grow up being measured all the time in comparison to a brother or a sister. **Our most important job as a parent is to not only enjoy and treasure the differences in our children, but to actually help them and guide them to discover who they really are.**

Frankly, that is one of the most amazing things to consider

in the make up of a family unit. I have never understood how from the same sperm and egg combination that we all turn out so differently. One is quiet. One is funny. One is taller. One eats fast. One is smarter. On and on it goes. My belief is that at the magic moment of creation, the dice go flying and NOBODY knows where they will land. I know there are studies about the middle child thing. However, none of these rules work all the time. We are each so unique.

Imagine then if you will, the frustration and loneliness in being told that your parents wish you were more like someone else! We cannot be like someone else. We end up being who we are. Happiness comes from being loved and supported for just who we are. Our parental responsibility and challenge is to help find the uniqueness and character differences in our children, and then celebrate them with each child. I guess that's the curve ball my mom threw over the center of the plate that day in the car. I missed hitting my selfish home run emotionally, but learned the value of a parent that worked every day to cherish the differences in her children.

The same concept again works in the business world. The best manager finds out what unique talents lay inside each of their employees, and then uses those talents to maximize the energy and effort of each person. In the professional sports world, the example couldn't be clearer. All the athletes at this level of sport are finely tuned and trained. Yet, championships are won by organizations that find a leader that gets inside the heads and hearts of its players. It is almost as if the leader says, "There is nothing I wouldn't do for you." When the team really plays as a team, not just individuals, it is magical to watch the result. Have you noticed how the word **FAMILY** starts showing up in post game interviews when the champagne starts flowing?

Chapter Two

Showing You Care

The Path

One of the most important ways a parent can support a child in the early years is to make sure the child believes that there is nothing more important in their life than attendance at all the activities the child is involved in. I cannot count the times I have heard my adult friends and acquaintances remark that no one ever came to their games or school events. At our house we called those people "the drop-offs." **The doubt that is created by this one action can affect a child for the rest of their life**.

I don't believe I ever missed a game or a school conference in the early years of my children's lives. There really isn't anything more important than that. It gives your child the absolute confirmation that their life and efforts matter to you. Matter of fact, while you're at it, why not be the coach of their team. It is amazing what you can learn from watching your child interact with other children on the playing field or at school.

Frankly, there is nothing more fun than going on field trips with children. They can be so genuinely amazed by the simplest things. It gives you a perspective that you may have long ago forgotten. I remember one kindergarten teacher named Belle who invited me to go on a trip to the pumpkin patch at Halloween the year after my child was in her class! We had such wonderful day acting like kids with the children that she hoped I might like to come along again the following year. Is there a greater compliment to be paid? Not for me. It was unfortunate I didn't know sooner and had a scheduled trip already or I would have gone for sure.

The trend continued at school. My favorite teacher was Mrs. Staroskie in my son's third grade class. She found my enthusiasm refreshing and would invite me in to read to her class often. She also let me raise the big plastic gavel on the Reading Auction Day when the children could bid on prizes with tickets they won for reading books. I taught them how to get excited when bidding on an item they desired. We practiced raising our hands wildly in the air and going "OOOOH, OOOOH!" It made them all smile to see they could actually get away with making a little noise and having some fun in the classroom.

Apparently the enthusiasm I showed in the classroom was appreciated by Mrs. Staroskie. She continued to invite me until my third grade son was in seventh grade. You see, he was my youngest and I wasn't ready to finish with grade school quite so quickly. The connection ended when in the following year she dropped back to teach second grade. I told her I was uncomfortable with having to learn a whole new curriculum. She laughed. I still get the biggest hugs when I see her.

Once in second grade, I was invited by Mrs. Murphy to come in and read to the children. As I entered the classroom, Mrs. Murphy happened to notice that I had on my size 13 high-top red tennis shoes. OK, I know they might have been easy to see. She asked, "What do you have on your feet there, Mr. Trayser?" Somehow the answer came out of me quickly, "Why Mrs. Murphy, these are my reading shoes!" For years after that I was known around school as the guy with the red reading shoes. It became a trademark of mine because of the notoriety it gave me. I even had parents call or come up to me in town and ask why their child wanted to have red reading shoes. I said that if that is all it takes to have your child be more interested in reading, wouldn't it be worth it to track a pair down now? They usually agreed. I now own seven pairs of red shoes and happen to have on a pair at this very moment. They make me run faster, jump higher, and seem to bring a smile to people's faces every once in a while. What can it hurt to stay a little child-like as we get older?

I would love to have a federal policy established that allows for parents to take a half day off without being docked for pay. Frankly, I think it should be mandatory for all parents to spend a full day in the classroom once a year as long as the kids are in grade school. The long term affect of more children believing their parents cared could be startling. The sad thing is, the parents who need to be there the most are the ones who rarely make the effort to show up. It seems to be a circle of neglect that begins early in a child's life. If you don't sit down and read with them often, they may be behind other students when they start school. If you don't help them with their homework, then they can fall behind and have a hard time keeping pace with the other children. My wife is a first grade teacher who can tell who is getting support at home and who isn't. Why is it not surprising then, that as the early years go on, that these are also the parents who don't attend conferences or go to games?

You wouldn't believe how hard a job that teachers have. If you haven't tried keeping the attention of thirty first graders for an hour, let alone a day, you owe it to yourself to see what it is like. I have always said that teachers deserve to have their pay tripled and at that they would still be under-paid! They spend more time with our children than we do during the school year. Why wouldn't it be smarter to pay them so much better that we attract the absolute best people to care for our children's early learning years?

The children see other parents at school and activities and have to wonder why their parents are not there as well. Give me one good reason or activity that is more important than supporting your child's effort at school or on the field. There simply isn't one! If your reason is that your parents never supported you, then you need to ask how that made you feel? If it made a wall instead of a path, then you are at a crossroad that will confront you for the rest of your life. **Is it time to break a chain of behavior that hurt the growth of your own self-esteem? Learn from the things that you didn't like and make an effort to change them! Otherwise we continue to elongate the chain of dysfunction** that you know is hurtful and unhealthy. Everyone loses when that happens! That is when a wall is broken down and the bricks are used to build a path instead.

The Wall

You want to make a child uncertain about your love? Don't bother sticking around for their soccer game. Don't bother going to school conferences. Don't help with their homework. Don't go to the play they are in. Children are more aware than you give them credit for. I developed an equation years ago that may be appropriate to share at this time:

$$\text{Love} = \frac{\textbf{Support} + \textbf{Empathy}}{\text{Time}}$$

Time

Walls are created by leaving out parts of this equation. If you don't stick around for the soccer game, you miss the opportunity to share the excitement of a victory or the disappointment of a loss. You also miss the knowledge that comes from watching the interaction of your child with others. This can play a big part in making judgments as to how you can help guide your children's effort and attitude in the future. If you are off getting a cup of coffee and a paper, you miss the point completely of athletic events. **It isn't always about winning and losing.** It is about the effort you make and the interaction again of a team sport. You can learn a great deal about your child whether it is on the field, playground or in the classroom. **But first of all, you have to be there.** Time may be the most important value in the equation. Without it, everything else falls apart.

The empathy part of the equation plays a very important part as well. This is the part of life where sharing your history and ideas about winning and losing come into play. The wall can be created even if you are there. Many of my adult friends have shared stories where they played as hard as they possibly were able and their parent ALWAYS had some comment that made them feel smaller. That usually happens because a parent had unfulfilled dreams from their childhood. It can be a valuable time for guiding and sharing for a parent to share how they felt playing sports when they were a child. Mostly we are there to watch and support the effort that was made.

There can be a challenge for the family when too much pressure is put on a child during these public displays of effort. If too much pressure is applied, the child may not play to their utmost capability simply to refrain from making mistakes. It is a painful sight to see a child cry in public because of a parental backlash. Having empathy means cheering for the whole team and designing the goal of the day to play hard and HAVE FUN! My folks always said, if you can't say something nice and positive, say nothing. That is very appropriate for this type of event.

There is a sadness to hear an adult say that they over-achieved as a child simply to try and get the attention of parents who were drop-offs. The desire to gain that attention can continue into adulthood and spread across many phases of a person's life. We are all just children that just get older as life goes on. The desire to belong and be recognized for our efforts is a natural thing that is developed in our childhood and continues until the day we die. Support for our children in all of their activities and the empathy that lets them know we care, can be a wonderful way to bond in the early years. You just don't get a second chance at childhood. Help them make the best of it. Remember, we were all children once. How would you have liked to be supported? There is where the best answer lies. Live your life with no regrets.

There is one more part of the equation. Time in its cumulative form is a concept that needs to be evaluated briefly. The very early years of a child's life are obviously the most important years. If for some reason, no one stays at home to care for the child and they feel the time portion of the equation as a negative affect, there can be serious repercussions down the line. Let me share one more field trip story. You know you have done something right in your life if your child invites you in their freshmen year of high school to go on a field trip with them. I have been told by many parents that they are more often invisible to their child in those years and that their children usually deny having parents at all. Well, my son invited me to tag along on a trip to the local atom accelerator laboratory. I have to admit I was curious about what went on over there after having driven by it for years. It certainly was a great transition from a trip to the pumpkin patch! The honor of still being included at this time in my son's life meant a great deal to me. As we made the short bus ride, I saw something that annoys me on field trips. I see the parents all sitting together. I find it to be a great time to spread out and sit by children you don't know and chat them up a bit. You will be amazed by the things you will hear them say. It surprises them that you seem interested in their answers.

It really upset me as I overheard a conversation later that day on the way home from one of the parents. She said very clearly, "I can't wait until my kid leaves for college." I have a very strong feeling that the child is fully aware of those words and their meaning. If you haven't used the time together at home properly and a child's departure is looked upon as a good thing, then you have wasted those impressionable years. Talk about a brick wall! That statement drives a stake right through the middle of my heart! I have been deeply saddened by the departure of my children as they went off to college. It is one of my best friends leaving town for god's sake!

Let me state this very clearly. If you have spent your years in search of greater monetary levels in search of more stuff and a bigger house, and you have a poor relationship with your child, then you have failed at the one thing that can be looked at with pride in your later years. There is no second chance at parenthood with your children. The only legacy that you leave on this earth that REALLY matters is a happy, confident and unconditionally loved child. Take one more look at the above equation and see how your efforts can be focused on helping your child see and believe how you care for them. If you don't have their attention and friendship started by the time they head off to grade school, then it will be harder for them to excel in every phase of their future. I am afraid I know of many adults that are still trying every day to achieve the acceptance that they so desperately missed during their formative years. Let them know you care! Don't be a drop-off parent. Sign up to be a coach or volunteer at school while you still have the chance. The reward for you and your child will be priceless in the years ahead!

My final measuring stick regarding this point is very simple. You may want to write it down somewhere. **Spend twice as much time and half as much money on your children.** You will both be better off with this rule!

Chapter Three

Hugging and Kissing Your Children

The Path

Physical contact with your children is a very important part of the bonding process. From the first day at the hospital, to every day you are together at home, a connection can be made that will last a lifetime. In my book, it is clearly an extension of my "there's nothing I wouldn't do for you" philosophy.

Let me tell you another story. There is a cumulative effect to much of what we do with our relationships. If you begin your child's life by holding them close whenever you have time for it, you will find it a natural process as time goes on. My dad was a big hugger. When he whipped that smile of his on you and held out his arms, there was no way we could keep from running into his arms. He was our hero getting off that bus every night after riding the train home from the city.

He was also a big kisser. We were kissed by our pop until the day he died at age 86. That bonding moment always felt right and good to me throughout my life at home. I saw that not many other guys kissed their dads, but that never mattered at our house. It was a natural thing for me to continue with my boys it seemed. Well, one night a number of years ago, we headed into town to exchange cars with my college aged son. In the car were my Colleen and a good friend of hers. We were headed to a hockey game. We turned into the gas station at Four Corners and pulled along side my son's car. I jumped out and when JC saw me, he bounded out of his car, threw his arms around me and gave me a big smooch right on the lips. This was always the way we did it. We quickly exchanged keys because we were late. As I climbed back in the car, I heard sniffling in the back seat. Our friend had tears rolling down her face. I had no idea what had happened that might have triggered that event.

I asked if she was alright and through her tears she said she was fine. After regaining her composure she said that she had never seen that level of an emotional connection between a father and a son. It made an impression on me that still rings true tonight as I met my Jared in Minneapolis as we head to our home in Montana. I was telling sweet Melissa, who was sitting next to me on the plane, how excited I was to be connecting with my son tonight as he has been away at college. As we walked off the gangway together, she saw the face of this good looking kid light up. He threw down his backpack and purposefully strode over to me and lifted me off the ground and then planted a kiss or two on me. Right there in the airport with people all around. You should have seen her smile, because I had told her that I felt like the richest man in the world because of my relationship with my boys. The confirmation of the following hugs and kisses let her know just how glad we were to be together!

All of this emotion is a cumulative effect of our friendship over many years. From the day I first held him upon returning from the hospital, to the many nights I stood and rocked him back to sleep after a feeding in the middle of the night. To the cozying in the big bed on a Saturday morning or sitting many nights together reading his favorite book together. It's funny, the things that make a big impression on you some time. A few years ago, just before Jared went off to college, let's see, that makes him 18 years old, he was in bed and as I bent down to gently touch his head and give him a good night kiss, he looked up right into my eyes and said, "I love it that you still come in and tuck me in at night, it means a lot to me." Holy Cow! I had no idea the impression that simple act made on him. Again, it was a huge connection for me and made a big impression on the cumulative timeline that had stretched out over those 18 years.

I was simply doing what my parents had done for me all the years that I lived at home. Each night as they would come in to say goodnight, they would always end the moment with these simple, comforting words, "Angels watch over you." That emotional hug was something that closed the day's activities down with a gentle, positive feel to it. A day doesn't pass where I don't say that to one of my children or someone on the phone.

I'm not a religious man, yet it feels right to say these words, in that it might give just a second of comfort to someone in need.

I would like to suggest that this hug and kiss thing is a VERY valuable bond. I am very confident in saying that over the years, in discussions with women, that they feel that a man who is gentle and kind is clearly more virile and strong than his counterpart who thinks hugging is for wimps. Guys, if you want more loving from your wife, treat your kids with gentleness and respect. I guarantee you will gain their admiration. And, oh yeah, it doesn't hurt to love your child, just like that! The macho, tough guy thing helps no one. The path that we create for our children and friends, by wrapping our arms around them and letting them know how glad we are to be with them, is a beautiful thing to behold.

I even have a hugging barometer. You can tell how warmly a person was treated as a child by the way that they hug. I see three basic styles. First of all is the side hug. You know, where just as you go to put the hug on someone, they turn to the side so that you bas into their shoulder. It is a deft move when executed properly and is very hard to defend. The awkward moment it creates for me is confusing. It was like they weren't that interested in receiving my love. That person didn't get much touching or hugging as a child for sure. I try to make a mental note of that moment and register it in my head so that I can work up a strategy for the next attempt. Sometimes I can make it happen even as we say goodbye by using some of my Jedi Master, hug moves. I will use the force, if absolutely necessary!

Hug style number two is the shoulder hug. That is where, as

you start your hug move, the defender hunches their shoulders down so that you don't get a full hug. You get the shoulder collision. It is a very popular move with women who don't want to give away the secret that they have breasts on the front of their bodies. I know a couple of women who have mastered this move and I have not yet found the angle to overcome it.

The last hug move is of my own creation. You are going to love it! Promise me that the first time it works for you, that you will drop me an email that describes not just their reaction, but more significantly, yours. Here it is. First, you need to see the magic twinkle in the eye of your quarry. You know, that moment when you can see that someone is REALLY glad to see you. Then, after you give them a good hug, you pull back without letting go, look them in the eye, and say, "give me another one because I'm so glad to see you." You won't believe their reaction! It solidifies how honestly happy you are to be with them again. There is no greater confirmation of friendship!

I need to share one more story that made a lifelong impression on me. My success as a businessman came from one very simple idea. I treat EVERYONE like family. My competitors were always amazed at how I ended up staying at the homes of my clients. Typically, after visiting the San Francisco home office of my company for a few days, with me as host, you either got the "John Trayser thing" or you didn't. My personality may be overwhelming for people that are not used to a great deal of positive energy. Well, the next time I visited the client in their hometown, they would automatically invite me to stay at their home so they could treat ME like family. It was an awesome response to my effort on their trip out west.

Upon scheduling a visit to a client in Louisville, Kentucky, Mark asked me to stay at their home so I could meet their sons Blaine and Ross. You see, I spent a portion of the time together out west talking about how lucky I was to have the family I did. Sharing funny stories about your kids is a great icebreaker and you can learn a great deal about someone from the way they talk about their family. He and his wife were great people and had a fun time being with me for those days together in San Francisco. So I gladly accepted. After our meeting at the office and a round of golf, we headed home. Gina was there to greet me with a big hug at the front door. Behind her were these cute little boys peering around her to see who mom was hugging. My guess was that they were about 6 and 8 years old. Most client relationships would have just the adults going to dinner. I always tried to include the children. We all headed out for pizza. I am sure there are times that I act more like a kid than an adult. I always try to sit at the "kid's table" at any gathering. **Frankly, I think this adulthood thing is overrated.** Anyway, pizza was the obvious choice. We had a bunch of laughs and I probably entertained the kids as much as the parents.

By the time dinner was finished, we were all laughing out loud. It wasn't too late yet as we arrived home. With the boys all wound up, the three of us ended up on the floor wrestling around and playing with some of their toys. Mom and dad just watched and shook their heads at the three boys on the family room floor. Then it was off to bed for the kids. Mark, Gina and I talked some more and the evening wore down with a cozy, family feel to it. It's times like that that make me feel like a lucky man. Making new friends, doing some business and getting paid for it. Thank God I never got the guilt thing working. Off to the airport and another client began the new day for me. How much business someone did with me was never the point. How good of friends we turned into was the measuring stick I always used. By that standard, I am the richest man I know. I am even Uncle John to some of my client's children. God I love being on somebody's refrigerator!

A few weeks later, Mark called out of the blue. No business, but a serious voice. Here is what he said, "It has taken me three weeks to get the courage up to call you. I needed you to know that you have changed my life. When you were here, you got down on the floor and wrestled with my boys. I grew up in a home that was very formal. My father never wrestled or played with me like that in my life. It looked so good to me, that I have started to wrestle with my boys, and it feels great! I just needed you to know how grateful I am." It knocked my socks off! The things I took for granted from my childhood were newly treasured by someone else. It is definitely one of the best sales I ever made. Oh yeah, just so you know I am not an angel, he later said, "you didn't happen to use the word butthead while you were here did you?" Apparently the boys had recently added that word to their vocabulary. I did confess I knew that word. Maybe he was still happy with me because of the balance. Ha, Ha!

It is clear to me that we all are hungry for the friendly touch of our parents. It is a basic hunger that we all share. When in doubt, I always throw a little love around. To not do so jeopardizes the part of our heart that needs to develop in our early years. Give your child that one more important brick that will be used for generations to come. I can tell when a man hasn't been hugged by his father. It pains me to see the void where the love has poured out of a broken cup. Don't let that opportunity for such a basic reinforcement of your love go unused. It can be such a fabulous connection! Given the ONE COMMANDMENT, what would you choose? Remember, if you are doing something that was done to you, and it feels wrong, it is. Make your children feel safe in every way you can. It is really the only legacy that counts.

The Wall

I have an interesting question for you. If you could change any one moment in time, what would you change? My answer to this question came very quickly and easily. I would have God, or any of his associates, strike down with violent hell fire, the first person who crossed the line of physically or more specifically, sexually abusing a child or any family member. It actually gives me doubt about this God thing. How could a just and caring God allow these ultimate travesties to occur?

My understanding of this problem is limited, but I believe that abusers were usually abused themselves. I would like to introduce a concept that fits throughout the circle of relationship building that I believe in. It is called **THE ONE COMMANDMENT.** I believe that the religions of the world could be simplified greatly by the use of this concept. I don't know if one commandment jumps into your mind, but it might. **DO UNTO OTHERS, AS YOU WOULD HAVE THEM DO UNTO YOU.** All the other commandments fall into place when you look at it from this angle. Using this logic, is there ANY excuse that you could give, that would permit someone to think that any kind of abuse is acceptable? Any excuse?

This family unit should be the ultimate circle of trust. When that trust is violated, it is the hardest hurdle imaginable to overcome. I have been told by a number of people that they go to bed every night expecting something bad to happen to them. Is there any great curse to put on another human being? If you are abusing someone, stop it right now! Hell was created to punish abusers I hope. If you know of someone being abused, help them in any way you can. There are many health related organizations that can help these families. I serve on the board of one of these called The Friends of Child Advocacy. What is painful about this board is that we get involved only after the cases are brought to the court's attention. What I pray for is a way to keep the abuse from happening in the first place.

If you have abused someone, it is never too late to get on your knees and ask for their forgiveness. It allows each person involved to at least find a new avenue of thought that may give some relief to the parties involved. My goal is to find a way to eliminate the Jerry Springer type of show that legitimizes the dysfunctional family. When people view that type of insanity, it makes them think it must be okay to perpetrate that behavior, because other people are doing it.

Violence begets violence. Each time you raise a hand to

someone, you can count on the result being that violence down the road will be more possible. Try using heartfelt words to make a point before you raise a hand. With the One Commandment at your side, would you want someone to raise a hand to you to make a point? The bullying problem at schools these days has to be a direct result of things going on at home. No child left untouched will have the desire to physically or mentally abuse someone else. I have seen fathers, when "playing roughhouse" with their son, actually **play** hard enough to actually hurt their child. My belief is that this is a result of that father's dad using his power to make the child afraid so that there would be no doubt who was the stronger of the two. There are better ways to establish respect in a relationship between a father and a son.

Instead, we should help our children develop a vision that allows them to watch over others. We should teach them to laugh with others, not at others. There is no good reason to belittle any other human. It is typically done for one simple fact. **There are two types of people in the world. There are people that help others in any way possible to become stronger and there are people that make others feel smaller, so they themselves can feel bigger.** See if that doesn't ring true the next time you see someone attacking someone's heart, mind or body. You will see the absolute nastiness of that act more clearly and hopefully have a reaction that will defend the person being attacked. It is a very good feeling to help another person in this situation. **Remember, bullying begins at home. Don't blame the schools for the problem!**

Chapter Four

Using Your Mirror

The Path

People often say to me, "John, I just love being around you. I'm just happier when I'm with you." After the first few times that happened I started to wonder what was going on that made that happen. What I discovered was that it wasn't me they were enjoying. It was being with someone who liked them for just who they were. It was the mirror I held up that showed them the reflection of what I truly liked about them. If you stop and think about that for a minute, you will see the logic of why that makes so much sense.

My parents held up a mirror for each of the boys to reflect what they saw, that made us each so unique. Some people are uncomfortable with using their mirror. It usually comes from a lack of confidence. Giving someone a direct compliment doesn't come easy to people who are uncertain about their own self image. Matter of fact, it can be even more difficult to accept a direct complement. For that reason, I'd love to share a great trick I discovered by accident over the years. Here it is. The next time you hear somebody say something nice about someone, remember what they said and put it in your pocket to use at just the right time.

Here is what happens then. The next time you see that person; you take the words out of your pocket and share them with that person. What that accomplishes is threefold. First of all, the person receiving the complement is not embarrassed by the boldness of a direct observation about them. Secondly, the person realizes on an indirect basis that you must also feel that way or you would never bother to pass on the words. Third, you score some huge bonus points for the person who originated the compliment and may have solidified a piece of a future relationship between those two people. Man, is that awesome! At our house we introduce that by saying this line, "somebody said something really nice about you behind your back." The next time you see an opportunity to say something nice behind someone's back, go nuts and give it a shot. You will love the smile it generates.

The birth of self esteem starts earlier than you can imagine. From the first time you are held close, the tone of the voice you hear and the sounds that emanate from the household, all affect your early development. When you hear the same voices cooing over you, there is a calming and consistent pattern that allows for comfort to become a pattern. All of these feelings are the beginning of the mirror that will shape the child's self image as the years roll along. It is a constant barometer of well being or confusion.

Maybe because I was successful as a businessman, people often come to talk with me about their job situations and career paths. I find a consistency to how the time together goes. I ask a couple of questions and the individual will enthusiastically tell me exactly why they are the right person for the job they are seeking. At the end of this discourse they **always** say the same, exact words, "okay, what I should tell them at work?" I tilt my head and smile in disbelief. For some reason many people feel that saying nice things about themselves is just outright bragging. No, that is simply confidence. Convincing yourself that you are right for the job is an essential part of the process. The enthusiasm for any part of a business transaction or convincing your parents about something you need or want is way more than half the battle.

Here is a classic example of what I am talking about. My sweet daughter-in-law Sara came to me after graduating from college to talk about the interview process. We had spent many hours together over the years talking about life and its wonderful intricacies. So I had some keen insights about what made her tick. I gave her some of my impressions from my past experiences in the corporate world. In the end I basically shared that what she needed to do was to let her spirit shine through during the meeting. **An interview is only a short sales call with you as the product.** She is an accounting major and saw the subject matter as potentially unexciting. However, she has this bright spirit that strikes you immediately upon meeting her. Because there wasn't much harmony in the home as she was growing up, she had difficulty in believing what she had to offer a company was something special. That is so sad because this is one very bright lady. There was no mirror for her to see the reflection as she matured. For me it was easy to see what value she would bring to the corporate environment. She was a hard worker through school and always lit up any family gathering with her sense of humor and easy laugh.

I knew she wasn't totally convinced, but she had grown to trust my observations and I had some credibility by raising a great son to love her just how she needed. She had gone through a short process with an executive search firm and went off on an interview with a very well known name in the corporate world. She had learned that she was competing with nine other individuals for the position. She was a bit uncertain about how the interview had gone when she called to give me a quick play by play of the meeting. I wasn't all that surprised when she called a few days later to tell me that she had just heard from the company with an offer to immediately start in the position. She was big time excited when she called because they had told her that it was her SPIRIT that had sold them on her interview. You see, you can train anyone to be an accountant, but you can't train someone at work to have spirit or be a team player that will make the FAMILY at work pull together. They knew, as I knew, that their office would be a better place for having her light shine there on a daily basis. That holds true today, a few years later. Sara will go as far as she wants in the business world simply because she believes in who she really is today.

Here are a few phrases that will help you create a positive mirror image for someone:

1. Have I told you what makes you so special?
2. How did I get so lucky to have you for a daughter?
3. That was a great effort in your game today!
4. Did you know that you have a great smile?
5. I sure was proud of you today!
6. I love going to teacher's conferences about you!
7. You make a great big brother, did you know that?
8. You are going to be a great leader some day!

Do you get the point? You are simply reflecting the things you see in front of you, but saying them out loud leaves no doubt. That is what the mirror is about; creating a self image that has no cracks in it. You can tell your children over and over how you want them to be. What you find out in life is that they end up being more like you than you could have possibly imagined. So let's be careful of what we reflect at home. **The ultimate way for a child to build their self esteem is to have two parents treat each other with great respect in front of them.** Marriage is not always a honeymoon. We all know that. However, if your tone of voice is sarcastic most of the time because of issues you have with your spouse; don't be surprised if your child carries that trait on in his/her attitudes. If you show little respect for the effort others make; don't be surprised at your child growing up making cracks about how their friends just don't measure up to their standards. We really are mirrors every day. Start paying more attention to what you reflect and you might be surprised at what **YOU** see.

My parents always had a kind word for other people. My dad used to freak out the checkers at the grocery store by calling them by their names on their badges. He was the friendliest man I ever met. Everyone had something nice to say about my dad. I'm not sure as I think about it today that he even knew or realized the power he had. He just thought it was easier to be kind. I remember going on errands with him on Saturday mornings. My favorite stop was First Federal Financial in Chicago Heights. It seemed as if a halogen spotlight would go on the moment we walked in the door. He knew every teller's name and they all beamed as he walked up to the counter. What is truly amazing to me is that the employees of my bank have now grown to appreciate the smile, spirit and attitude of my sons as they have grown old enough to do their own banking. They always tell me at the bank how thrilled they are to see those smiles coming through the front door at Cititbank. The mirror I saw all those years ago has carried right through two more generations. I wonder if those folks at Financial Federal knew that my dad banked there because they had coffee and donuts in the lobby?

When my dad retired, my parents moved to the good life and warmer weather of California where my eldest brother Charlie lived. My dad took his magic with him I found out. He was always amazed at how the people at his new bank were always offering him box seats to sporting events like he was some big

contracted cancer and in a matter of a few months was withering away right in front of everyone. He had looked so strong the first time he had appeared at our front door. It was a painful time for all of us. Yet, Jonathan was down the street almost daily. We hadn't seen Uncle Dave for some time. JC (Jonathan) had come down with a case of pneumonia in the last month and was looking very pale still. As we went around the table his turn came. He said, "I'm grateful that I only have pneumonia and am going to feel better some day. It looks like Uncle Dave is going to die soon." We all heard the pin drop. And the tears fall. What a thing to be grateful for. He is still that caring a young man. In his training class at his first job, he was ranked 1st out of 65 fellow trainees. He faxed me a copy of the memo of congratulations from his regional director with a note he wrote on the bottom of the page. He wrote, "I blame you for this!" I was the emotional equivalent of Bill Gates the rest of the month and still remember it today.

Mr. Wilcox took to heart the mirror that sat at the edge of our kitchen table. The next time in town he stayed with us again. JC had some serious issue to discuss about something going on at the High School. David sat in rapt attention as he listened to JC's discourse. I fairly quickly had formed an opinion and made my position clear. All of a sudden, out of the blue, David's hand shot straight up in the air and he started waving it like a flag in a strong breeze. We all looked over at him at the same time since we had not seen anyone quite so excited at our dinner table. I said, "Yes, David." He said, "Can anyone speak here at the table?" I said, "Of course you can. We treat you like family and you act like family, so you can participate like family." The funny thing now is that I don't remember what he said or even what the subject was. All I remember is two things. The pleasure he showed at having his opinion matter at the family council and the eyes of the boys as I said that I had not considered that angle of the matter and that I changed my mind about my opinion. Did I see David light up with pride? You bet I did. Here was a thirty-something man getting the buzz that should have been part of his childhood development. Yet, you have to figure his dad was treated the same way as he grew up. Was his tail wagging as he left the table or was that just a joyous swagger in victory at the Trayser table? Yes it was. We are all hungry to have our opinions matter, regardless of our age.

For those parents who feel that children should be seen and not heard, you need to re-adjust your brain and take to heart how much our children can teach us if we just get our adulthood thing out of the way. If we show our children that we value what they say, they will start to establish their own identity and opinions. This template will determine the direction of their own philosophy. We always listened to their answers before cutting them off. Sometimes we agreed and sometimes we disagreed, but always valued their right to have an opinion. **Frankly, the only answer I find totally unacceptable is, "I don't know."** I believe that you always know. You either know or don't want to say what you think, or you are nervous about what others might think.

Do you remember the Dr. Wayne Dyer book, "You're OK, I'm OK?" I always joke that the reason I seem so happy is that I am working on a sequel to that book. It is titled, "I'm OK, You're All Screwed Up." People usually laugh at the concept but I don't really intend it as a joke. I don't think I ever read the book, but I imply that if you spend all your time worrying about what other people might think of what you say, you often don't say what you really think. I take opinions and discussion very seriously. There is nothing more fun with your clothes on than some intimate conversation about things that matter to you. Frankly, I feel it is the best foreplay. Sometimes intimate conversations can come from times and places that will surprise you if you keep your antennae up for the opportunity.

I was working at Continental Bank in Chicago when the oil and gas department hit the fan. A number of people were violating some very serious loan policies and had extended credit where they shouldn't have, on a wholesale basis. It took a federal bailout to fix the transgressions. I was working for the Trust Department at the time and we became valuable to the lending officers at the bank because we could go out with them and talk with their clients about something other than lending. This sweet veteran of the bank, a wise Irishman sought me out to travel to visit some Wisconsin clients with him for a full week. It can make for a long week if you don't like someone. However, he was the classic Irishman with a big smile and laugh. Our dinners together were a riot and serious at the same time. He was many years my senior and found my enthusiasm refreshing and my opinions hilarious. What he was most amazed with was how I didn't change my wit or style when we were on our business calls. I will never forget the last call we were on. It was a late Friday afternoon at Menasha Paper Company in Neenah, Wisconsin. We were meeting with the Chief Financial Officer and his staff investment director. For some reason, maybe because we were a little punchy from a long week's worth of calls, I had three of them in stitches. Okay, I know it may have not been totally professional, but if you can have a good time while working, then you have earned many bonus credits on the clock of life. Well, at the end of our meeting, my associate looked across the table and said to these gentlemen, "I need to tell you that I have had a most interesting week with this young man. I have never met anyone like him. Yet, after many long nights together in conversation I need to let you know something about him. He is lighthearted, not lightheaded." The clients laughed and said that they had enjoyed our hour together more than they should have and that they were grateful we had brightened a fairly dry subject. I took that statement and put it deep inside my front pocket to take out and look at when someone felt I had crossed the line, as will sometimes happen. It became a life statement for me. I give you the right to use it if it fits your personality or situation in life. My Colleen has used it from time to time because it is a perfect match. Lighthearted, not lightheaded, is a fun way to live.

My parents allowed their mirror to let me develop this way as I grew up. If they had given me the seen not heard thing, there is no way I would have had the success I did in business. Of that I am certain. I guess that is why when I started to hit home runs at the bank and afterwards at other jobs, I always called to blame them for my success. The ability to have confidence in a face to face meeting or beginning a new relationship with someone you just met is an amazing gift to give your child. If you have to choose between leaving your children a pile of money or the ability to be confident in their own skin, go with the latter. It will pay big dividends and feels a great deal more rewarding to them.

The other very important part of the development mirror is that if a child is guided properly, they will find out who they really are as time goes on. What this does is maybe a parent's most significant contribution to their child's welfare. When a child develops his/her own identity, then they have the capability to present to the world who they really are. This is so important! It allows them to present to schoolmates, friends, co-workers, girlfriends and their future spouse an accurate picture of what they are like. Those children that are not allowed the freedom to develop their own self identity due to parental capping of thought and feeling spend the rest of their lives trying to change in a chameleonic manner to fit in with everyone. This can be very painful to watch. As an aside, I have seen this occur often in young men/women we call Trustifarians. That is someone who was given a great deal of money at a young age and for some reason they lose the value of creating their own self image because the road has always been paved with no bumps in it. My old friend Jack Moses used to say, **"The measure of a person is how they act when they stumble."** So, when things get tough at work and you know you've been treated unfairly, state your case clearly for your family to hear and attack the problem with dignity and positive attitude, not angry retribution. Yet, if you don't let your children fall and learn life's lessons on their own, then they will fall very hard and have difficulty when the hard times come. Jack used to laugh at me and suggest that I got myself into some crazy situations just to see how I could find my way out of them. That is not true Jack, I think. God rest his soul. He always took time for me when times were tough.

One of the only times I had serious, unhappy words with my mother was in regard to a friend of mine. Charlotte was a great friend in high school and played in a band of girls I managed. They were called "The Distractions." And they were distractions! What a great name! I dated a couple of them. They played of Jefferson Airplane's "Surrealistic Pillow" because of the Grace Slick thing. Anyway, Charlotte's parents were known to be heavy drinkers. My mom one day actually forbid me to go and hang out with Charlotte because of her concern about the diligence of the parental units at her house. I felt strongly that she was mistaken. Yet, I know for certain that my mom would have done absolutely anything to protect any of her young ones. We had words and I remember going out to the front yard and cutting down a dead cherry tree that needed removal. It was vengeance chopping for sure! In reflection, I'm not sure who was right or wrong in this case. Sometimes you have to let your children make decisions that they feel closer to, even if you are wary of the outcome. That day, the defense of my friend who was in need of friendship was more important to me. My mother and father had also taught me the value of loyalty and I believe loyalty won out that day.

After murdering the tree, I remember disobeying my mom's wishes and scuttling over to Charlotte's house since she had a row with her folks and I needed her to know she could count on me. I didn't stay long. Just long enough to let her know how much I cared about our friendship. For god sakes, we had listened together, in the dark, while lying on the floor, to the Beatles White album! She even had filled in for our drummer at one Sock Hop when our drummer George couldn't make the gig! She was my best friend at the time. You have to be able to count on your best friend. This entire story leads to one complex fact. **Parents are not completely responsible for our children's self image. However, we are responsible for monitoring who our children have as friends.** When our children were grade school age we went out of our way to meet the parents and see the environment where they would be playing. The full circle of life came about for me when we made a decision to not let our child ride or play with one child whose father smelled of alcohol all of the time, including daytime. As your children become high school age it becomes almost more important to keep tabs on who they hang with and where they are. It certainly becomes more difficult as they begin driving. Yet, it is even more critical because of all the temptations available to kids these days. My sons all tested our ability and trust by not being where they said they were. All you can do at that point is make them aware of how disappointed you are and focus on the subject of respect. Without it, we may as just give up caring and that you simply must not and cannot do.

By the way, after heartfelt discussion with my mother, I convinced her that she needed to trust me on whom and when I should have as friends. I still am in touch with Charlotte. I will say this for my mother. She had a very strong personality, but she was ALWAYS fair.

As I write this paragraph my brother Dave is on his way out to Montana to spend some time fly fishing with me and our new drift boat. He is even more excited about coming to spend time with our new yellow lab puppy, Trigger. He fell in love with our other two labs, Gibson and Marley some time ago. Now that he is retired from a successful coaching career he has time for this type of foolishness. I can't wait for him to arrive! I wanted to make one final point about the path that our folks laid down for us. The bricks they laid were always unconditional. Even though Dave got all the athletic talent, big time national champ NCAA type baseball talent, he also got all the humility. I was Player of the Week for basketball in the local south suburban Star Newspaper in 1968. You'd think it was Olympic Gold the way I have played it up over the years! He is the best brother a guy could ever have. He was the one who went to meet my mom at the airport and let her know that our newborn little girl Megan was in trouble and probably not going to make it. Maybe the hardest job in the world, but he did it with grace and sorrow for his brother John who just couldn't find the strength to do it.

I describe a bit of our difference to make one last point about the magic and mystery of the mirror. Confidence and self esteem come in a variety of flavors. After meeting me and then meeting Dave, you would never guess that we were brothers. He has a QUIET confidence that showed up in the most amazing way on the baseball field. He was the field general and everyone knew it. This quiet guy once even told the coach in college to quit bugging his pitcher from his position behind the plate. It was a definite Jekyll-Hyde moment that made a huge impression on me. There is nothing quiet about me. I have had more than a couple of people point this out over the years. **The point is this, self esteem and confidence are shaped in many different ways and are molded to fit the inherent characteristics of the individual.** Don't force a square peg into a round hole because your first child was a round hole.

My eldest JC is our quiet one, Jared is the intense and driven one and Austin is the free spirit. They all carry that confidence thing very well. Not the bragging kind, but the watch over others kind, that people point out to me on a regular basis. It is a source of great pride for me and I simply say thank you, but I am jumping up and down inside. If there was any comment I would take back in all of my parenting years it is this; "I wish I could be more like Austin." I simply meant how sweet it looks to be so free of spirit. He's a great deal like me but without "the edge." People have always been drawn to the light spirit he gives off so easily. Of course I see pieces of myself in each of my boys. I hope I give off the genuine kindness that emanates from every pore of my JC. He is the gentlest person I know. I know that Jared has intensity that makes me look weak willed at times. Yet, his little boy heart can bring you to your knees with the way he watches over the rest of the planet. I'm afraid it will be his greatest strength and weakness for all of his days. I pray he finds a balance within his intensity. If he joins me some day on the speaking circuit as we have been discussing recently, he will make me famous with his personal power. May you all find half the pleasure and reward that these bright lads have given me.

59

They make me look good a little too often and it has been a joy to build a path for them.

The Wall

I know you can reflect back to your formative years and beyond into grade school the general feeling of comfort or distress that existed around your house. I feel it is safe to say that if your parents argued a great deal, then you may still have issues regarding face to face conversation. Many people view ALL direct conversation as confrontation. Worse yet is watching your parents treat each other with a stark coldness. There is nothing worse than feeling the ice forming between two people who you are around every day. The ultimate loneliness in life is being with people you love and yet feeling alone. Have you been there before? I believe I read that in Dante's "Inferno." It was the description of hell. The more I considered that idea, the more it scared me with its truth. Being simply alone is mild by comparison.

I use the word **chain** very often in my speeches because I see all relationship skills and tools creating the chain of behavior. **The wall that is built between parents and children can often be a chain of unhappiness that is created by parents who are struggling with their own self identity.** I believe that this is the source of most of our problems with alcohol and drug addiction. Parents and children who find themselves wallowing in the cesspool of unhappiness created by low self esteem is maybe the most vicious and damaging brick I know of. If you do not make a conscious choice to eradicate this unhappiness in one way or another, it will take you down. Sometimes slowly and sometimes quickly, the walls are built so high that one gives up trying to see over or around it. If you do not have temerity or genetic coding in some cases to attack the darkness created by the walls, then suicide looks to be the only way out. Why else would you kill yourself, if not for the simple relief of continual shattered thought?

It takes a very concerted effort to begin the war against the original construction of a family wall. And make no mistake, it is a war. The opposite of that war is surrender. Then life becomes dull and prodding with time being killed, not used as the gift it really is. Intense analysis is part of the potential destruction of the wall. Yet, without the first step of making a choice to break the chain, the effort will falter. I have seen the physical and emotional pain that is caused by the choice to not attack the wall of darkness. It looks like someone is carrying a cross or burden that is so heavy that it is impossible to find joy in any facet of one's life. That also feels like a description of hell on this earth.

The mirror that creates a wall instead of a path is much bigger and stronger. You may agree with me that it appears to be much easier to be cynical, not hopeful. It appears to be easier to be sad, not happy. It appears to be easier to be complacent, not driven. Are all of these choices we make? I believe so. I came up with an anagram for this problem. I called it ICE work. Intensity, curiosity and effort are the words. Without all three working together at the same time, you are destined to fail in your war. It takes a concerted effort to be happy if you did not see happiness in your house. I have seen people try and fail. I have seen people just not try. I have seen people make the effort and overcome the darkness in such a manner that you feel like standing and applauding the victory. **Those who do tear down the wall seem to appreciate each day even more than those who were given a path to walk on. The effect seems to be driven by the distance between the edges of the bell shaped curve that they worked so hard to overcome.**

There are some very simple things you can say that will build a wall between you and your children. Here are a few:

1. Please go have a sleep-over somewhere else.
2. What do YOU want?
3. Why can't you be more like your sister?
4. I can't wait until vacation is over and you go back to school!
5. Why should I go to your conference, they will just tell me how bad you are.
6. I can't wait until you go to college!
7. Forget going on a family vacation, that is too much time together!

All of these reflect a mirror image of neglect in the early, formative years. If you don't build a path in the first 5 **(FIVE)** years of your child's life, then count on some heavy duty sledgehammer work to demolish the wall that has been built. However, it is NEVER too late to begin. You just have made your work that much harder. And certainly you have made EVERYTHING for your child that much harder as well. Learning in kindergarten, 1st grade and on forever becomes more difficult when your child is struggling to understand why they are not fitting in with the other children. If your child is having behavior problems on the playground during school, don't look at the teachers like it is their fault. You need to look at what has gone on at home.

If you have spent the bulk of your time in the evening camped out in front of CSI Whatever and not reading to your child, then you have started building a wall as solid as the Berlin Wall with children on one side and adults on the other. My guess is that you won't bother to attend any conferences at school either. Any time you are about to blame a teacher at school, stop and look first at how much time you have invested in your child's DAILY life. It is a cumulative event this wall and path thing. There is a conscious choice to be made. If you feel that having a bigger house and a hot car is more important than the future of your child, maybe it is time to re-examine your priorities. If your childhood could have been different and gave you a better feeling of love and security, wouldn't you do everything in your power to make it happen for your child? It doesn't have to be mom that stays at home. A loving and caring father will also fit the bill. These formative years lay all of the groundwork, foundation and the first row of bricks for either a wall or a path. Make the most of them and I guarantee you will NEVER regret the time you have invested.

Just use the analogy of starting a business. If you don't lay the groundwork in the beginning and let your business be run by someone else, what have you done to the chances for the business to succeed? If you spend all of your time at work and leave the child rearing to a nanny, day care or babysitter, what have you done to the chances of your child feeling loved and worthwhile? There will be plenty of time for empire building when your children hit the ripe old age of five and are on their own at school. If you don't buy any of this, please do me a favor. Go to ANY grade school. Find ANY first grade teacher. Ask them if they can tell which children are being cared for and helped with reading at home. I don't doubt what the answer will be. You see, I helped type report cards for my wife for many years. As the editor and typist on the job, I could feel the difference in the comments being made. **Honestly, I think the lack of parental involvement is the biggest problem we face in our schools today**. Just ask a grade school principal what they think of this statement. I am fairly confident that they would agree.

Chapter Five

The Chain

The Path

If you have felt the victory of tearing down even a piece of the wall, I applaud you. If you are still considering the choice and are wondering whether it is worth it, you need to spend a little time with my Colleen. She is a warrior who has won the war and people are drawn to her spirit because of the joy she so freely gives to everyone around her. She is living proof that the war can be won.

Do not give up. Time is too precious to be wasted or killed. **Reach out in any way you can find to start the war against the wall that has you fearful, full of doubt and without hope. Your parents did the best they could. Forgive them. Break the chain of sadness that permeated their lives. Your children's lives, your life, your community and the world's cohesion**

are at stake. I couldn't be more serious! If you do not make the effort to break the chain, you will perpetuate the agony of sadness that you see in the eyes of your children when they see **you** so unhappy. They need the connection with their parents to become fully functional human beings. It would be easier for them if you were not there. To be so close to someone who gave you life, and not have the complete path to your heart is almost criminal to me. There is no excuse good enough to convince me that it is not worth the effort. If you are so uncomfortable with a face to face discussion of the heart, write a letter telling them how you feel and how you got there. I don't know if it holds true for you, but I would rather know bad things, than be left in the dark knowing only silence. When that happens, we ALWAYS assume the worst. You have to be able to able to lift the pen. Yet, I know it must weigh a ton or you would have done it by now.

Let's go back to our old friend, the ONE COMMANDMENT. If your crippling sadness has made your life so miserable that you cannot find joy, why would you EVER inflict the same lonely heart on someone else? Rise up! Find just one person you can count on. It may not be a professional at first. Simply look for someone that you could trust to hold your heart for a minute or two. The next time it will be five minutes, then ten. The biggest step in the process is the first step. It might appear to be the Grand Canyon, but if you never try how will you know what the thrill of freedom of heart feels like. Are you going to go to your grave with a deep regret that you didn't try or try hard enough? Consider the upside...

Now that I see these words coming together, let me share an

amazing story with you that will demonstrate what the other side of sadness looks like. You may be inspired to take that first step at the end of the story, so hang in there with me. I was told by a marriage counselor that my wife was just not interested in being "best friends" with me. It was the fourth marriage counselor we had tried. I was just looking for an interpreter that might make clear why I was so lonely even though I was married to a beautiful woman and had three fabulous boys. I know we appeared to be the "Beaver Cleaver" family to the outside world. That made it even harder. I knew her family situation and realized that her dad had finally beaten me. He was a cold man who found it easier to be kind to others, but rarely kind to his two daughters and wife. He never went to anything they were involved in. He had no sense of humor which made it difficult for us to be friends. He turned away from me the three times I asked for his daughter's hand in marriage. Frankly, he had crippled their children's hearts. With the professional's words and my wife sitting right beside her, I finally gave up trying to be best friends. Don't confuse that with me not being in love with her still. I was. But sometimes you do have to know when to fold them. The mirror was cracked and all the duct tape in the world couldn't fix it. I guess I was slow to catch on to what she had been trying to tell me for quite some time. But I saw my happiness being sold down the river with her dad at the helm. And now that he was dead, there was not much hope of fixing things. Bummer….

I moved to our vacation home in Montana to plan my next move. I could work out of there easily with a phone and a laptop. As fate would have it, the night that Cal Ripken broke

Lou Gherig's record for continuous baseball games played, I met a very interesting woman. She had this big spirit that came across the other side of the bar like a lightning bolt. After I sang "God Bless America" three times beginning to end, she invited me to join her for a game of pool at the favorite local saloon. We put our quarters on the table and waited our turn. I happened to notice there was an abundance of real cowboys in attendance that night. You know, shit on their boots and dirty hats. Real cowboys with dirty pick-up trucks parked outside. As fate would have it again, we were unstoppable. I think we won like 13 games in a row. With each victory we became noisier and I am sure more annoying to the cowboy crowd. We finally figured out that we better lose one and hit the road before there was bloodshed at the Old Corral. We hooted and hollered only after we were outside. We were winners, but not stupid. She said that she and her friend would come over for a hot tub, but didn't. I was surprised they didn't come, but understood. I was a few years her senior. A few days later, I was leaving the same saloon after lunch with my fishing buddy Kim Ratliff. Colleen was sitting on a picnic table with her friend Shannon. She later told me that she had just finished telling her friend about this UNUSUAL man she had met the other night. It freaked her out that I had appeared at that moment. We ended up partying a bit together that night and I remember Kim and Colleen dancing in a parking lot to my favorite blues guy, Robben Ford, under the stars with my car stereo serenading us. She was a riot and nice to look at too. But it was always her spirit that kept my rapt attention. Full of life I guess you could say.

We started hanging out together after she finished work each day. The evening always ended in the hot tub. No sex, just intimate conversation about our lives. It turned out that she had some serious ghosts from her childhood that would never seem to go away. Her parents were both drinking with a vengeance and the family had chipped in some money for an attorney in hopes that they might get a divorce. I guess that means that the nine kids were desperate. She was number eight.

My mirror was still very intact from the unconditional love that my parents had given me. I held it up as long as I could each night in the magical healing waters of the hot tub. She told me I was the first person who ever took the time to ask so many serious and heartfelt questions of her. She was like a sponge and would show up the next night with twenty more questions. It appeared to me that her parents were never interested in her activities at school. Sometimes they even forgot to pick her up. Frankly, she was raised by her older sisters. This is something I couldn't relate to, at all. Here is where the whole story has been headed. All this other stuff was important background. But the deconstruction of the wall had started right in front of me. I just didn't see it until I was putting all these thoughts together for this mirror thing. I have told this story before to people, but I didn't see the significance of what I am about to share with you.

At a certain point every evening, after the tub thing, we would move into the tiny living room and continue the conversation. After shaking off some of the tears and pain of earlier conversation, Colleen would get to a question that would make her so uncomfortable that she would jump off the couch, run down the stairs, jump in her car and drive home in confusion. She had hit the wall. It might be a day or two sometimes, but she always came back. Then the same thing would happen again. She would jump off the couch, run down the stairs, jump in her car and drive home. I could see the wall in her eyes. That she came back at all was at first a surprise, but I could see that she was extremely curious at to how I saw things fitting together in her life and I had no other hidden agenda. This went on for about three weeks of intense conversation. Then the most amazing thing started happening! She would run into the wall around her heart and head for the door, run down the stairs, jump in her car, start the engine, sit for a few minutes, turn off the engine, walk up the stairs slowly, open the door, look at me with tears in her eyes and quietly come and sit down on the couch. Damn if I didn't see a huge brick crash right down next to her on the couch! The first brick had been battered off the top of the wall! I could see it! And she could feel it! The tone of the conversations started to change after that, brick by brick. Don't get me wrong. It wasn't as easy as I am making it sound. She was the one doing all the work. I simply found her curiosity enthralling. What I didn't see at the time was, with every brick she knocked, no, blasted off the wall, I took and lay down in front of her. A path was starting to be constructed between us. Wow! What a buzz that was for us! We at that point didn't care all that much that the whole resort town was talking about us. We were at war and at this point we were not taking any prisoners.

She still had moments of jumping off the couch, running down the stairs, jumping in her car, starting the engine, driving away, but then not making it all the way home. She would turn around down the street, park her car in front of the house, come up the stairs, open the door and throw TWO bricks against the wall near the fireplace. I would pick them up, mix a little mortar and then place them very securely between us. I don't know if either one of us knew exactly what was going on. She was a bright star for me and she was just the friend I was looking for. Her metamorphosis was as exciting and beautiful to watch as that of an emerging butterfly. It took almost three full years for her to believe that I didn't have another shoe to drop and that what she was witnessing between us was simply unconditional love.

That was ten years ago. She says I saved her life. I know she gave me a second chance at love that I never thought I would have. I thought about this story last night and whether it was appropriate for this book. This morning after re-reading it, I feel strongly that it is an important part of THE CHAIN. And here is why. Sure it is a love story. But it is also a story of hope, because the chain has now crossed over from my family to hers. I swear to you that Colleen said that all of a sudden, the trees were greener, she could actually see the striations of the bark on the trees, and she was listening to conversations differently and talking differently with people. She felt free! She no longer thought bad things were going to happen to her each night as she went to bed.

But something else had started to haunt her. It snuck up on her from behind when the fog had cleared. She was mortified that she had been a bad big sister to the only other person below her in the chain, her little sister Toni. There were many tears shed over the wall she had built between them. I believe she even used the word mean. The psychological term for this behavior is displacement. That is where you pass on the pain someone is giving you because you have reached the overload point and can no longer hold it in. It has to go somewhere and the natural process is to the next sibling in line.

After seeing and believing that a wall could be destroyed and a new path put in its place, I thought Col was ready to try it with her sister Toni. She was reticent at first and I knew she was very nervous about reaching out the first time because of the sadness she had caused. On top of that, if there were any conversations with the other sisters, and there weren't many, they always ended up talking about what a bad time they had growing up. It hurt to listen, but things were about to change for the good. I think we started the path by sending Toni an airplane ticket to come and visit us in Montana. Her husband was in the Navy and was gone for long stretches at times and it seemed like the perfect opportunity to get together. I am sure that there was time spent on the phone while the mortar was being mixed to start the path. Col may have even gone down there first. But what is REALLY important is that the first step had been taken. **Remember, it is never too late to start to tear a wall down or begin building a path.** Over the next few years I saw a miracle in front of my eyes. And make no mistake, it is a miracle. Trips to see each other became more frequent. Phone lines were heated up with conversation. Sure, sometimes the past was discussed, but you could feel the amount of time spent on the past diminishing. Col even found the strength to simply apologize for being unkind as a big sister. Believe it or not, a HUGE piece of the wall fell at that very moment.

Then another miracle started to happen. The other sisters started to get in the loop. The chain and path was forming. Walls were coming down. I remember just sitting there listening sometimes and frequently found myself grinning. Col would have to start with the past with the other sisters, but she knew that good things could happen if she kept taking down bricks and laying them as a path. Now Col was really getting wound up. Years had gone by. The sisters were spread out around the country. Colleen started forming a master plan to begin the complete reconstruction of a chain and demolition of the wall that had been around for her whole childhood. At this point Col was around thirty years old. A lot of walls can be built in that amount of time. But by this time she had become fearless in her assault on the past.

The plan was this. They would all throw caution to the wind and let their families know that they were planning a SISTERS TRIP to Key West, Florida in February. I'm sure there were some surprised husbands and kids. Airfares were compared, hotels were searched, a van was rented and the ASSAULT ON KEY WEST was completely organized. Col was giddy. That is the only word that comes to mind. Giddy. I don't know if I helped in any way, but I had told Colleen about a few family gatherings that I had planned over the years, including getting all my cousins and their families together for no good reason except to celebrate the family ties we had enjoyed growing up. They were great memories to hold on to as the aunts and uncles died off one by one.

There was only one ground rule that I insisted upon and it was made clear down the line. The first night together, they could yell, scream, bitch and holler about the past all they wanted to. They could even get drunk and rowdy about it. Then, the next day, the future would be discussed. Sounds like a path forming to me! Go figure. They had a blast. Hotel, bed and breakfast, van, dinner, the pool, drinks, you know, carousing. I could hear the buzz all the way across the country. Not on the phone, I mean I could hear the sisters all the way to the mountains of Montana! Col was in heaven. She was rebuilding her childhood by remembering some events from the past that were good memories that had been covered up by all the pain of the walls that were built. She once said to me, "You have helped me go back and enjoy being six years old again." I swear to you this is true. Could I possibly given my new best friend any other gift that could be more treasured? I could feel my mom and dad smiling down on me for passing on the chain that they had given me so unconditionally.

This is not "Love Story." There is no unhappy ending. This is power. This is love. This is hope. The story just gets better. Sister trips have become a tradition. Here's a picture for you to envision. They planned a houseboat cruise on Watts Barr Lake in Tennessee. Activities were planned, pirate bandannas were purchased and eye patches were worn. Sounds like sisters enjoying their childhood to me! Damn I was happy! There was a whole new side to Colleen that I had not seen before. She used the word ecstasy to describe her new found joy of life and sisterhood. Now they talk ALL THE TIME! I can actually hear the tone of voice change when a sister is on the phone. My favorite it is that Col and Toni and Barbie all finish each other's sentences. It makes me laugh out loud to see them together. Picture them together, trapped in a small hotel room in Kentucky during a massive storm with thunder, lightning and rain that had washed out Barbie's son Aaron's baseball game. The energy I heard over the phone was far greater than any storm could muster. They are hilarious together.

Being of the Catholic faith, there was one problem. I was not divorced. I had been separated for a few years by this time, but my wife and I had agreed that for the safety and comfort of the children, divorce could wait. There are so many bad connotations to that word that we were just trying to reduce the pain for our children. We still enjoyed parenting together. I had simply been honest all along with my three boys and told them that I had a new best friend. That logic may be simplistic, but outrageously honest and true. That is a whole different book in the future.

I'm sure that I appeared to be Lucifer, the Devil and any other name you can manufacture, to her family. I wasn't invited to family birthdays, etc and I understood why, sort of.

Then another miracle occurred. Sister Tina took a risk of lightning hitting her and decided to come out on a family vacation. Maybe behind the scenes, they had done scissors, paper, rock and she had lost! Anyway, Tina and her husband and two children came out during the summer when my wife and boys were there also. We had a great time. Everyone got to do whatever they wanted and laughs were a regular part of every day. The two children had challenges. One was autistic and the other had Tourett's Syndrome or something like it. What Tina hadn't counted on was that my boys have huge hearts and have always watched over other children with kindness and grace. A great time was had by all. Big hugs were shared as they left. But what followed upon her return was the miracle. She apparently spread the word through the family that yes, John's separated wife and boys were all living together with Colleen and John in Montana. We did have the advantage of plenty of space and privacy for all. But what she said was this, "I don't know why it all works out there, but my children and my family have never been treated better by anyone than by that Trayser clan."

The clouds were parting, the earth was shaking and I was no longer the devil. A few years went by with happiness being spread around left and right. Then the story gets better. Two years ago, the first ever family reunion was held in Michigan. I was invited and a great time was had by all. Family pictures, stories, a card game called Tonk, time at the beach and plenty of food were shared over the 4th of July weekend. Now I'll tell you that I am not sure that all of these events were the direct result of Colleen tearing down the wall between her unhappy childhood, but it looks like a new chain has been created in her family. The only sad part of the story came just before Christmas this year. Her mom contracted stomach cancer and died in less than two weeks. We were grateful that her suffering was short. The sad part was seeing the clippings and notes about love and family that her mom had hidden in the pages of a book that the sisters had found while cleaning up her things left in her condo. She had so wanted to make her children feel safe, but just didn't know where to begin. At the private family memorial service I could see how badly every one of the children would have loved to have heard the words from their mother directly, not hidden in a book. As the eldest sister Linda read the words from the clipping, I could feel the mom's spirit hanging like a cloud in the living room. I am afraid the cloud was filled with regret.

I remember Colleen telling me the day she fell in love with me. She was sitting at the restaurant where we met and she worked, with her then boyfriend, tennis pro, Steve. I had just won the town's doubles championship and was in a great mood celebrating with a few friends. Somehow I started telling stories about my boys, since they had been at the match. Colleen and Steve were not sitting with us, but at the bar. I had bought them dinner because the duck I bought in the fundraiser had won and I had earned $80. Steve had suggested I buy the duck chance and my policy is to repay a kindness with a kindness. **She had told me that as she listened to my passionate voice sharing kid tales, that if she thought that her dad had felt that way for just five minutes in her life, she would have given the world for it.** The sad thing is, a few of her dad's friends came up to her at his funeral and said how much he had talked about his daughters. What was it that kept it from going from his lips to her ears as a little girl? The chain of loved not shared during his childhood is where I would look first.

That is the feeling that enveloped the room during the memorial. Opportunity lost. Love held close instead of thrown around. **The reason I share this story is a simple and direct one. I do not have a degree in psychology, family counseling** or related fields of study. However, I have seen the direct effect of unconditional love. It works. It works miracles. It is the only way to achieve a life fulfilled with love and the only way I know for you to go to your grave with NO REGRETS!

Chapter Six

No Little Kindness Is Ever Wasted

The Path

When I was younger, I admired wealth and cleverness. These days, I admire kindness. I read something like that a few years ago and it stuck with me. My parents were two of the kindest people ever put on this planet. A day didn't go by where they found some way to say something nice about someone, or do something nice for someone, without being asked.

That legacy goes a long way in describing how my boys have made such a great effort at watching over other people as they have grown up. My eldest son, who was ranked 1st out of 65 trainees, had one client write his company with this story. She was in the middle of having her car towed for the first time in her life. It had just quit working and she was very disturbed about feeling stranded when the tow truck came to take it away. My son arrived on the scene to find the lady in tears. Now, company policy doesn't state exactly what to do in that situation, is my guess, so after identifying himself to his client, he simply said,

"Mam, it looks like you could use a hug." She was so surprised at his compassion, she slumped into his arms. She just needed someone to show they cared about her distress. I found out about this when my son forwarded me an email from a regional manager who received a note of thanks from the client. I couldn't have been more proud. **It is not always about the money we make. It is about the relationships we build as life goes on.** It works the same in a family as it does in business. Strong customer service people probably had a great support group at home as they were growing up.

Again, most of the training time for this kind of attitude takes place in the first five years or so of a child's life. There is definitely a cumulative effect to the ability to reach out and be kind for no good reason to someone. My middle son was just on the phone from college and I told him where I was in re-writing the book you are now reading. I asked him what he could tell me about the kindness thing that might help people understand the importance and simple act that can make each day brighter by giving a helping hand. He said that most of his friends don't understand the kindness thing. He believes that there is a certain level of insecurity in people that makes them worry about what people will think about offering up kindness in many situations. They seem to choose the "I'm better than you" attitude that appears to be the easy out for not lending a hand.

Let's point out a few classic examples. My most favorite is related to the travel world. How many times have I seen someone struggling on an airplane with a carry-on bag that they are trying to put in the overhead compartment? It might be a girl, a father, a son or daughter or a teacher after a rough day at school or someone still stunned by and oncoming divorce. It just doesn't matter. If someone looks like they need help, get off your butt and help them. What if it was your mom struggling? Wouldn't you want to have someone jump up and help her? That is how simply I view this very important subject. This is the first step to creating a better world. I am very serious! If you can make this effort to help someone, maybe someone else will think it might work for them. On my last trip to Montana, on a Northwest flight, I saw about ten rows away a young woman trying to figure out how she was going to fit her bag in the overhead compartment. There were people in the aisle in between us, so I didn't know how I was going to be able to reach her for assistance. Just then a young man jumped up and grabbed her bag, and with one easy movement put it in between two other bags. It's funny to see how many people are watching this happen and never make a move. As we got off the plane I caught up with the young man and gently grabbed his elbow to get his attention. I simply said, "That was very kind of you to help that young woman with her bag." He gave me a broad grin and shook my hand. He said, "It doesn't seem to happen often enough, does it?" It is the little things that can count. **Please, the next time you see someone struggling with a bag, jump up and help them, you will feel**

better for it or even thank someone else who beat you to it. Wouldn't that be a subtle beginning of world peace?

Here's where it started for me. This is classic Trayser behavior. You are on vacation in some wonderful place, maybe Disneyworld. You see a family about to take a picture in front of Space Mountain. This photo could be so much better as a Christmas card if the whole family was in the photo. My dad would always run over and offer to take the picture for them. This may appear to be a very small gesture. Yet, I know that it makes everyone happier, not just then, but when they get home! The whole family together! Do you get the significance of that? If we would all act like one big family, the world would be such a better place to live. There will be times when they say no thanks. It hasn't stopped me from continuing the practice. They will often immediately offer to do the same thing for you as a return favor. Usually, they at least say thanks with a big smile on their faces. I typically just suggest that they pass on the favor the next time they have a chance. It is the classic "pay it forward" move.

Years ago while on a trip to California, there was a young couple on a beach north of San Francisco. We were the only other people there. As we walked by I offered to take a picture of them together. They said that they didn't have a camera with them, but that it was a nice thought. I offered to take a picture with my camera and send it to them because they looked so sweet sitting there together. Then they hit me with a ton of bricks. She said that this was their last time together for a while because he was going off to jail the next day….oh my god! I did follow up with sending them the picture when we got home. I have often wondered if they were still together. No little kindness is ever wasted.

My dad was very big on bringing my mom flowers. Rarely were they for a special occasion. Usually it was just because he was thinking of her. It made a serious impression on me. Anyone can remember Valentine's Day, but where were you in July when it was hot and humid and the kids were driving you crazy because they were out of school? That seemed to be when my dad showed up with flowers for mom. I stole some of dad's style and one year I raised it to a whole new level. My folks had moved to California after dad's retirement. It was my birthday and I had decided after seeing my first child born, that it was a great idea to send my mom flowers on MY birthday. Think about it. Doesn't that strike you as a great idea? Well, that year I decided to give a better surprise than usual. I arranged for a meeting to be held at the home office about an hour away from their house. I flew to San Francisco and rented a car for my week's effort. I drove across the bay to Fremont where they lived. I got a big bouquet of flowers and a big Mylar balloon and parked in front of their house. I got on my cell phone and called my mom and asked if the flower shop had delivered the balloon to the mailbox in front of the house as my birthday gift to her. She walked to the front of the house and drew back the curtain. And there I was, leaning against the mailbox with a huge grin on my face, giving her a little wave. Thinking I was back in Chicago, you can imagine the shock on her face. The flowers were not that important on that day. It was the crying, hugging and jumping that I remember. By the way, the next year I had the flower shop deliver some flowers with a big balloon that said "It's a Boy!" on it. The card read, "Thanks for your help 40 years ago, Mom! And dad, thanks for your help 9 months before that; you big stud." They said the young high school aged girl delivering the flowers was blushing and giggling as they opened the door. No little kindness is ever wasted.

If there was one lesson I had to point to in my life that was learned by example from my father, it was this. **The genuine kindness and attention you pay to people you don't have to be nice to, is the real measure of heart in a lifetime.** I find that people are actually surprised often times when you start a conversation with them. My next story relates directly to this idea. One of the best sales I ever made in the investment business had nothing to do with money. A client name Cynthia, who became a great friend, paid me the ultimate compliment one day. Here's the story she told me. One day, she was heading toward an investment meeting inside the bank. She ran into one of the senior investment executives, a twenty year veteran of the firm, at the elevator. They started some idle conversation as they headed to the same meeting. By the time they had traveled a few floors via the elevator and hallway, she had said hello to five or six people. Just before they entered the meeting, the senior executive gently took her arm and asked her how she knew so many people at the bank. She said that a friend of hers had suggested to her that success and happiness could be found by being kind to others, for no other reason than simply being kind to others each day. For that reason, she had tried it and found that it gave her great happiness to make people smile. She had made many more friends at the bank. It also made every one else feel better. What an amazing concept! When she told me this story, I had tears in my eyes. It may have been one of my best sales ever. Just one more person reaching out to others can make such a difference!

Not long after she shared this story with me, she was given another promotion. She is a very hard worker and is known for getting things done. I couldn't be happier for her. I wonder if there is an immeasurable factor that exists that may play a part in business decisions. Would you rather do business with someone with an attitude like hers or some unsmiling, just doing my job, type of person? I hope it continues to be part of her daily life routine. It can make a difference for anyone. This story happened quite a few years ago. Today, Cynthia's riches have grown far greater. To the amazement of her co-workers and me, she jumped off the fast track to the top and decided to cherish the early years of her son's life. She elected to stay home and build a path for him to walk on the rest of his life. This time only passes once.

One more flower story if you will permit me. I saw the impression that flowers given without a "special occasion" made watching my father over they years. On top of that, his being nice to those you didn't HAVE TO be nice to had made an impression on me as well. During my years in the investment business, I saw that it was mostly a male dominated business. I made an effort to go out of my way to thank the people in the home office that supported my daily effort in the field. The operations and administrative staff were of course underpaid and underappreciated by the sales staff. It typically goes that way. For that reason, I would frequently bring flowers to the staff with a hug and a thank you. Not big bouquets, often just a flower or two. It was my first stop after getting my rental car and always worth the effort. One day in the middle of a client sales meeting, a group of about seven sweet operations/admin ladies interrupted the meeting to present me with a big bouquet of flowers and kisses. I was flabbergasted and honored at the same time. Apparently they had been grateful for all the times I simply made the effort to thank and remember them for simply doing their job.

It has dawned on me over the years that families work in a very similar way to corporations. Those families/corporations that make their members feel valued and cared for seem to have a much greater chance of succeeding and thriving. Those that worry about how others are doing or what others have that they don't, stumble because they have not paid attention to the small factors that allow their employees/children to grow. The more you invest in training/guiding your employees, the longer they will stay with you. The same goes for children. My folks have been dead for some time now and I miss them dearly. A kind and giving parent should be missed. I have seen the opposite where there is more relief than grief in a parents passing. You earn the loyalty of your children/employees by nurturing them in every way possible. Compensation is not usually the factor that drives an employee away. Eighty per cent of the time when an employee leaves a company it is because of the way they don't get along with their superior or fellow employees. Focusing on ways to support your children will make them better employees in the long run. Teaching them teamwork will make them leaders in a world that usually has everyone watching out for themselves, first. Kindness is something that there is no training system for. You need to have it develop as a byproduct of watching your parents treat each other with respect and then share it as you grow into young adulthood. **Remember, no little kindness is ever wasted.**

The Wall

There has been a great deal of discussion in the school systems in the last few years about the problem of "bullying." The obvious catalyst for the discussion was the horrific Columbine School shooting. It was unfortunate that the school officials didn't get wind of it until it was too late. I see the problem being the actions, or lack of action, by the parents as the children were growing up under their roof. Bullying is the exact opposite of kindness. Kindness is a good deed or action given freely for no good reason. Bullying is an unkind act perpetrated against someone for no good reason. The ONE COMMANDMENT immediately comes to mind here. Would you like to have someone give you a hard time because you were smaller or just not part of the right clique? The obvious answer is no.

My guess is that children who are pushed around at home are the likely candidates for pushing that behavior off on someone else down the road. If kindness and respect are used to teach instead of anger or physical force, there is no way that a child will develop the twist that allows them to think that being mean is acceptable behavior. Here is the likely point in life where there is a chance to break a chain. My guess is that harsh words, physical actions and bad attitude add up to a recipe for long term abuse within a family's history. **If you have been mean or are being mean, stop and think for a moment if this is the legacy you would like people to remember.** It is never too late to break a chain of distress and unhappiness. Just take your child's face in your hands and look them in the eyes and say that you are sorry from the bottom of your heart; twice or three times until they don't immediately turn away. It will take some time to earn their trust again. Yet, they are hungry for your gentle touch and will forgive you.

There was a guy in our neighborhood, Tony, who must have been facing some really bad things at home. His idea of a good time was to take a homing pigeon and tie an M80 (big) firecracker to the leg of a pigeon and then let it fly into the air. Do you have that picture in your mind? After lighting it he had a grin on his face like he was getting even with something. I spent at least an hour one day trying to talk him out of it. I just didn't understand the entire idea/feeling behind the act of abject hostility to a bird that was innocent of anything worthy of this type of fatal demise. He finally got tired of my pleading and took the bird home. I doubt my reprieve for the bird lasted forever. His brothers were all twisted and angry I wished often that they would find the justice they deserved. As an older man now, I still feel that they were very much at fault. Now though, I realize that they were probably giving the world what their parents were giving to them at home. Do you see the circle forming from earlier in the book? These are the parents that never took time to read to their children. They most likely never showed an ounce of respect for each other or the children. You can bet BIG that they NEVER attended a teacher's conference at school. They failed at parenting. It is quite probable that their parents were just like the legacy they were passing on. I pray that someone in their family got fed up with the sad trail of anger and unhappiness and broke the chain. Otherwise, you can count on their children sharing the same painful events as they grow to adulthood. I guess that's why there are agencies, too many I am sorry to say, that deal with these families as they spin out of control enough for the authorities to step in and protect the children.

If you know of a situation where the children need protection, step up to the plate for them and find someone to help. Wouldn't you want someone to make the effort to save you if you were in the same confusion? Appearances do not matter. All that matters is the safety of a child. Do everything you can to protect them! Your reward will be here on earth.

The same way the children need protection, employees need the same support. A company is just a bigger family. There were a number of times in my career where a boss or co-worker was stepping across the line of propriety in their behavior towards a fellow employee.

Most often it fell under the category of making someone feel smaller so that the individual would feel bigger. If you know you feel right in helping someone, just do it. Good things happen to people who do good things. At least that is what my children tell me. Oh yeah, they hear that from me.

Chapter Seven

Manners

The Path

There are other simple acts of kindness that indicate an understanding of the One Commandment. One of my pet peeves occurs every day across the country. There is nothing like the laziness of humans who refuse to walk their shopping carts to the areas reserved for them. It leaves me with an impression that there are probably other areas of their lives where their lack of concern for others may be seen. In a crowded parking lot, when you are ready to turn into an open spot and you see a couple of carts sitting there, it usually ends in looking for another spot. If the first person didn't leave a cart, it becomes less likely that the second person would leave one. That is how it works in life. One transgression can easily lead to another. If you do leave a cart in the parking lot with your child along, do you see the impression it leaves with the child? It works the same way in everything they see us do. Most of their behavior is a direct result of the mirror reflection they see as they grow up.

Let's take another simple, painful example. Just who is it that is littering? My great hunch is that it is people who saw their parents occasionally toss something out the window of the car or chuck a piece of paper on the ground in a parking lot. The ultimate bad one is when someone dumps the entire contents of their car ashtray in a parking lot or at a stoplight. For some reason, littering shows disrespect for our planet in a way that really riles me. It is only abject laziness that makes this happen. Yet, I think it goes deeper than that. It shows that as a child was being raised, the parents showed a complete disregard for teaching the basic difference between right and wrong. You may think that I am exaggerating the point. However, we are the builders of paths or walls. On which side of the brick do you choose to make a stand when faced with right or wrong? Littering is wrong, period. If you follow the One Commandment to this point, what will you choose in the future? I can't tell you how often I have walked to the top of my driveway to get the morning paper and found a variety of bottles or cans, paper and other trash that has been tossed out the window of a passing car. People who think that it is alright to drink and drive are probably the same people who have no regard for someone else's front yard. Right and wrong does have a few grey areas I will admit. However, sometimes the difference is quite clear. Littering is wrong. If you have a can in your hand next time or a piece of paper, think about what it means to throw it out of the window. It just might be the first step in building a path of kindness to others.

It was nice of someone to come up with the concept of "beautification" of our nation's highways. You know the signs that say that this mile of highway is protected and cleaned by ABC Company? That's nice, it really is. However, I would rather have a $10,000 fine for littering. I have a strong feeling that littering might come to a rapid demise. It could make a greater impact more quickly in defense of a defenseless planet. Respect the earth like the Indians did and we would have a much better chance of leaving it a better place for our children's children.

One last act that I believe indicates a persons' nature is "guy thing." Ladies, you have only a latent reaction to this simple act of complete disregard for others. And I know how it disgusts you. I'm talking about men who don't raise the seat when they urinate. No one talks about it. Yet it is such a clear indication of how people are not watching out for anyone else in their lives. At home, I grew up with four boys, a dad and a mom. Our rule was that we ALWAYS had to raise the seat before urinating and TRIED TO ALWAYS REMEMBER TO PUT THE SEAT DOWN WHEN FINISHED! It is a simple matter of respect for others. As parents it is our job and only our job to instruct our children in any way we can. This also is a One Commandment issue. It is a respect issue that I have passed on to my children since the first day they stood in front of a toilet. Would you like to sit down on a seat in the men's room where the guy before you had just finished urinating without raising the seat or even flushing? No one does! I want to change the world as I said in my introduction of this book. Lazy acts like littering and toilet issues will absolutely lead to other acts of disrespect.

Respect for others reaches to these very basic elements of right and wrong. My parents made issues like these very clear. So much so, that I remember pulling my car over in high school and asking my friend in the passenger's seat to go back and retrieve the can he had tossed out the window. He thought I was joking at first, but I made it very clear that I was not. That is what my Colleen calls "knowing better." Who else is going to teach that to your child? Every parent has the responsibility of teaching their child manners. These are some of the basic issues that we need to imprint in our children at a very early age. The antithesis of kindness is disrespect. We cannot parent with the assumption that our children know these things. Make a daily effort to help them see the significance of respect and they will grow up with the ability to watch over others. If you don't, how will they know the difference between right and wrong?

Now that I am on my king size soapbox, let me share a few other simple ideas that can affect your children's lives way down the road. I can't tell you how often I have seen children come into our house and use poor grammar. I mean POOR grammar. It makes me think that the thread that I talked about earlier regarding reading to your children plays a big part in this. The path that you create by reading with your children runs right into the full sized road as they head off to school. It extends right into young adulthood. High school aged children that are still using poor grammar are facing a liability even as they graduate from college and head off to their first job interview. If you are a new parent, please make an effort to turn off the TV and spend some time reading to your children. The simple bricks you lay today become an important part of the road to success that you pray your children will have. **Love by assumption does not work.** You have to pay attention to the fact that habits and ideas that you develop early on in your life become hard to break. If you were raised by parents who never took the time to read to you, break that chain and start a new one. The payoff comes sooner than you think. You will hear in your first conference at grade school that your child is an above average reader. I promise you that! What a great head start for them to have. At our house we tend to help correct grammar of our children's friends in a GENTLE way that lets them know we care. You'd be surprised at the impression it makes on those children. And often times, you can see them stop before making the same mistake another time while in our presence. It is not a "better than you" thing, but a caring thing.

Another important manner to have is the simple "may I help you." Yes, I know children are basically lazy. However, every once in a while my boys would stun us with that sentence. I'm afraid that this is one of those "by example" actions that can make a difference. If I had occasionally seen mom hustling around to get things done, I might offer up a "how can I help you?" For some reason we guys seem to be much better with a LIST. Are you guys with me? I will work until I drop with a list in front of me. I just don't see the counters as dirty that often or the floors that need vacuuming. But given a list, I will make every effort to accomplish those tasks. The path that this leads to is embedded in your mind as you grow. It makes your children appreciate things that others do for them, mostly because they have seen the effort that you have made around the house to make life comfortable and clean for them.

This lesson was driven home for me a few years ago. A few years ago, my boys got tired of one of their friends who never said thank you after a meal or wouldn't lift a finger to help. They had seen that at his house he had no responsibilities to help around the house. His ability to see the need for an occasional "thank you" or "please" had fallen by the wayside because of how he was taught at home. Instead of just dropping him as a friend over this matter, they cared enough to take him aside and explain the importance of being grateful for the effort that was being made for them around the house. To our great delight there was an immediate change in the young man's attitude. He was actually hungry for this type of knowledge and I am sure more than a little bit embarrassed that this kind of manner had to come from his friends, not his parents. Let's make sure that we help our children in any way we can, to appreciate the effort of others. It is a path that branches out in many ways as they grow older.

One more manner issue that is easy to fix is that of table manners. I am truly surprised at the number of teenage children who come to our house to eat and do not know the proper way to hold silverware. Actually, it usually is just the fork. The baseball grip that most kids use is an improper way to hold the utensil. This is not life and death, right and wrong stuff. This is preparing them for their first job interview stuff. It is a hard subject to bring up to someone without embarrassing them. We usually talk about it after they leave and try to see if there is some way to present the information in another way. If you don't know the right way, get online and find out. It can make a difference. It mostly depends on who's watching. If it is a future boss, then it matters a great deal. Give your children every advantage you can. Who else is going to tell them?

One of the simplest things we can teach our children, that make a strong impression, is how to shake hands when being introduced to someone. Have you heard the saying, "you only get to make a first impression one time?" You would be amazed at the number of times that people said something about meeting my boys for the first time. Maybe it is because so few people make an effort to teach their children the right way to do it.

The first thing you do is to not underestimate how early your children are receptive to this type of learning. As soon as they are able to say their own name and stand up, they are ready. A good firm handshake is where we start. This is going to take a little practice, but it will be worth it.

The first step in a firm handshake is a good smile. That's right, a smile. It will all be for naught if you don't raise your head, look the person in the eye and say your name clearly and add a word or two like, nice to meet you! A firm handshake that uses the whole hand, not just the fingers is the ticket. It is not a contest of strength, just an indication of sincerity and warmth.

The first motion is a step forward. This says that you are really glad to meet the person, not just performing a duty. My dad's friends always made comments about the way we acted when we were introduced. But, little was left to chance in regards to personal relations at our house. If you have not actually taught your children how to do this, it is unlikely that they understand how it works. It is the same for love. If you have not taught your children how to give it, they may not have a clue of the significance of just how it works. That is what this is all about. **You should leave nothing to chance in the way that you share everything you know, that is important, in regards to communications with other people.**

These little things all add up to creating self esteem in your child. This is quite important and needs to happen in the formative years. It will last a lifetime and is so easy to accomplish. Pay attention the next time you meet someone for the first time. Do they look you in the eye? Did they take a step forward? Did they smile? Take in your reaction from that moment and think what is happening. Did you really feel that they were glad to meet you? A first impression is made only once! Give it your best shot and make sure your children have this head start.

There is a natural progression from the handshake to another very simple, common form of communication. Telephone manners are so easy to teach, but again many parents just assume that their children understand the right way to act on the phone. It is very noticeable to me who has been taught to talk on the phone and who hasn't. You need to practice with your children before bad habits are the norm. They need to speak right into the mouthpiece and most importantly, focus on the person they are talking to. There is nothing more disconcerting than having the person on the other end of the conversation talking with someone else.

You should establish a short answering sentence so little is left to chance if they should be the first one to answer the phone. By that I mean you should come up with what you want them to say each time they answer the phone. For example, "this is the Johnson's, Kelly speaking." This lets the person calling know that they have a good chance at actually talking with the person they are looking for. I know this may sound simplistic, but each of these little things add up over time to create a positive self image for your child.

Sometimes the teaching works in two ways. I was over at a friend's house one day when the phone rang in the kitchen. The mom answered the phone and began her conversation. As the conversation went on, her young son would go over to her and pull on her shirt to get her attention. She would just shoo him away and he would stop for a minute or so. But soon enough he would repeat this action. Two things are going on. The mom is being distracted which is tough on the person on the other end of the line and the boy is not being taught proper manners.

After watching this go on for some time, I squatted down to the boy's level and asked him what he wanted to talk to is mom about. He said that he wanted to go over to his friend's house. I suggested that if he really wanted to get his mom's approval to visit with his friend that he should try a new tactic because mom was obviously not happy with his current strategy. I said that he might walk over close to her and put his hands behind his back and wait until she had finished her conversation. I made it clear to him that no one likes to be interrupted when they are talking. Then, after she was done talking he should look right at her face and say clearly, "may I please go over to Joey's house to play?" You should have seen the look on the mom's face as this happened. A bright light went on in her head that I may have had something to do with it as she had seen us talking. I suggested it was never too early for a little sales training. Even at the age of six or so children respond well to suggestions in how to communicate better. The trick is that both parties win when you do it properly.

The last telephone courtesy is to teach your child to cover the mouthpiece before yelling out the name of the person that is being called to the phone. Again it is a little thing and is just a courtesy to the person on the other end of the phone line. Imagine that you are on the phone and your children are answering...are you confident that what you hear is what you want to hear? Just the One Commandment again!

Do you want a sure sign that you are on the right track with parenting? Here it is! Do neighbors ask for your children to be babysitters? I have three boys, not the typical sitters I believe you would agree. Each one of them was asked to sit for neighbor and friend's children. It just dawned on me that it may be the greatest compliment another parent can give. Trusting your child's welfare to someone outside the family is a benchmark for many parents. I am not bragging here, just giving you a fact to ponder. If you can see that your children are the most precious things in your life, then imagine the belief and trust you must have to ask someone else to watch over your children. The funny thing is, the dorm resident assistant at my Jared's college said that is exactly what he does still today. He watches over all the other students because of the way we watched over him as he was growing up. He is the same guy that the 3rd grade teacher pointed to, just ten years older. That is the legacy I have been working on all these years. Leaving behind three young men that are known for good hearts, and are the guys you can count on in a pinch has been my reward. Again, they are not angels and have fallen to temptation from time to time. However, they are the best friends I have and I count on them in ways even they don't know. Can a parent ask for anything more?

Chapter Eight

Communication!
Where It All Begins

The Path

Did you have a parent that you really connected with? Can you say why? My guess is that you had at least one parent that you found comfort in talking with. I mean really talking with. With me it was my mom. When my best friend and roommate died freshman year in college, she had the heart and time to help me heal. She was the one who took my face in her hands and told me there was nothing she wouldn't do for me. My dad was a most kind and generous, loving father, yet my connection in the deep emotional sense was my mom. Maybe that is why I have always found it so easy to talk with women. I have the rare male friend that likes to talk from the heart, but men usually see that as a weakness, not strength. That's another way I want to change the world. Kill off the caveman and start a whole new generation of caring dads!

If you want to be that mom or dad that connects with your children, you need to learn some basics. First, I believe it is NEVER TOO LATE to begin communication. You simply have to want it bad enough to catch up with time lost! I am sorry to hear how often that the death bed is where forgiveness is given and sadness is laid to rest. Today is the day you need to start if you want to not have the regrets that are the most painful feelings in life! At 56 years of age today, I can whole heartedly say I have no regrets in the area of family love and communications. Doesn't that qualify me as a rich man? But that is all looking backwards. Where do you begin if you are a new parent today?

The first place you should look is in your own heart. The One Commandment can be a VERY powerful force here. How would you have liked your parents to talk with you? You know what works and not works in communication with you today. If you don't like being yelled at, don't yell. If you like to have quiet time alone to find the best path to your heart, make time to be alone with those you love. If you find that a certain part of your house is intimidating when you are there, like an office, don't go there for conversations. Be fair with those that have lesser skills in communicating. Hold anyone that needs it, even if you are mad and not in agreement. Try to NEVER go to bed really angry...or hurt. **After scolding a child, make sure you hug them and tell them you love them before they go to bed.** Do anything to make others feel safe to come and talk with you.

Be the safe haven that everyone needs and desires. Try not to be judgmental in your answers; there are so many different points of view in an argument/discussion.

Sorry, I got carried away there… back to where to begin with little children. I'd love to be known as the Dr. Spock of the years beyond the diaper. So here goes how it worked for me!

Communication with little ones begins with non-verbal moments. From the arrival at the hospital on, the child KNOWS when love is being given. If you hold your child only when told to, the child knows. Can there be any more precious use of time than to gently hold a child that YOU actually created? You are potentially the richest person in the world if you get the connection between love and cuddling your baby. The amazing thing is, the moments only get greater and more whole when you get to say or hear words in conjunction with the cuddling.

If you think changing a diaper is only women's work, you are missing the whole point of parenting. A team effort is helpful for everyone involved in raising a family. Your spouse will be grateful for your help and your child will know your face from that very special angle. It's funny these days, when I find my boys hesitating to help me with something, I say loudly, "come on! I wiped your butt for years!" They are in their twenties now and seem to respond to that statement with great humor, but also understanding.

If you are planning on working 70 hours a week, mom or dad, and have a great expectation of your parental efforts, forget it! These formative years come only once and almost any nanny is not going to give the same attention/love that your child requires. Put the larger house on the back burner if necessary. I promise you that there will be regrets for the time you miss as your children quickly pass through their toddler years! Just look at the flip side. Do you expect your parenting effort to pay dividends if you are investing all your time at work? It's the same in reverse. If your priorities dictate spending that much time away from home or working while you are at home, do you really expect to have a close relationship with your child? Look closely now. **Is the reason you spend so much time at work that you want to have great success and the respect of others for your effort? Well, the parenting thing works EXACTLY the same way!** There is ONE HUGE DIFFERENCE! This moment in time only comes once, period!

You can look at it from the holistic corporate point of view if you'd like. If you truly want to grow a great company, where do great employees come from? I'd venture to say that you might want college graduates that have had the love and caring over the years that makes them the confident, strong and moldable bodies that accept training and guidance instead of insecure children that are filled with doubts that have grown since childhood. You can see it in the eyes at an interview of that person that is in front of you. Is a young adult your best candidate for growth of your company or would you rather spin your wheels with someone who is riddled with doubt and insecure? What kind of handshake did you get? Did they look you in the eyes as they introduced themselves? **Are you starting to see the circle forming?**

The same people you want to hire are the same ones you hope to raise. Don't expect all the other parents out there to create the employees you so desperately want. The best product you can manufacture as a parent is a happy and confident child! Don't spend 60 hours a week at the office in those early years. Measure your success by being asked by your children to go on field trips when they are in high school. I guarantee if you never went to anything while they were in grade school, you will absolutely not be asked to attend anything in later years. It just doesn't work that way. **Friendship, caring and connection are all cumulative**. If you buy this logic, and you know you have to because it is loaded with common sense, then you have to start out by **wanting** to hold that baby. That is where it begins....

There is a certain type of person that finds that immediate connection with their child uncomfortable. They are the grandparent that shows more love to their grand child than they did to their own child. They are the person who gives more love to the neighbor children than to his own. Do you know that person? Where does that come from? I believe it comes from the lack of connection all the way back to the childhood of that parent. When that connection is not made, there is a void that grows in the heart of that child that spans the universe. The void if not filled in other ways becomes deeper than the Grand Canyon. **The inability to show that heart to heart love can become an evil chain of sadness that can span generations. It is the opposite of love and the heart and head of that person remains so filled with doubt and fear that the chasm grows into pain.** *That pain is the birth of the dysfunctional family*. It can be very difficult to pierce the veil of a broken heart.

I saw my father-in-law melt into tears on a regular basis when my first son would run past him up the stairs and quickly do an about face and run and jump into his lap. He would then look right into his grandpa's eyes and say, "have I told you that I love you today?" You could actually see him shake physically. The tears were immediate, and tender. Other than those moments, I only saw his gentle side with other children than his own. I know he loved his two daughters, but he never made that clear in all the time he was alive. Growing up in the depression in Wisconsin had to be hard, but I have the feeling that he suffered more from the cold of heart, than the cold of weather or lack of money.

I asked for his daughters hand in marriage three times. I was brought up to do the honorable thing. Each time he turned his back on me and walked away. We never had much connection other than a heart to heart about the highways of Illinois. Only now years later do I realize he wasn't being mean or cold. He just loved his daughter enough to not want to let her go. He just was unable to communicate that to me. He thought I was too young and too foolish for his daughter. I know that. He never really looked to see if she was happy. I know I freaked out the family with all my laughter and hugs. It was something that just wasn't done in their family.

The problem for me became that I had expected my wife to be my best friend and want to share my heart and my desire for closeness. I never saw the clear connection between her relationship with her parents and the difficulties that it might hold for me. You see, I was in love. Marge was as pretty a woman as I ever met. Not pretty, beautiful. The problem was that she told me that was all she ever had to be as a child. The hugs were rare and heartfelt talk was non-existent. There were moments where I thought the wall might come down, but before I could break through all the way, she would beat me to it by building it up higher than before. I knew that there was a scared little girl inside. I'd seen a glimpse and just wouldn't give up on freeing her. I'm afraid with professional help from the fourth marriage counselor I was told that Margie just wasn't interested in the intimacy thing like I was. She was sitting there along side the counselor with tears in her eyes and nodding through the description of their two meetings. She had been trying to tell me for years that very same message. I just refused to believe it. From time to time, usually very late at night we would get close to the heart of her pain of intimacy. It usually ended with tear stained words that would start with the words, "my father never…." And then the words would stop cold and no mention of the discussion would come the next day or the next day. It hurt to see her so affected by the years of desperate longing in a childhood vacant of that connective love. It haunts her still today. My boys feel that same desperation of desire to connect with their mom. I know she can feel it and see it, just like her father could. However, it must look like the mountain is too high to climb. It is why I am not married to her any longer. She told me to please give up and find someone else to talk to. So I did. The hard part is, I still try to love that woman. She is the mother of my children and we still enjoy parenting together. I truly believe she has given the right hugs and words to those children she has taught and made a difference in many of her student's lives. She is a great teacher and you would want your child in her class. Like her father, I believe it is easier for her to give herself away to others than it is to her own children. It is that damn circle again. I have begged her to break that chain of loneliness and reach out to her boys. They try just like I did to hold her heart. She just won't let it go....

This story paints a picture of sadness. However, my boys are not quitters. They are still trying to connect with their mother. When tears appear they feel the same desperation I did. All conversation comes to a halt when the words, "I don't know" appear. There is no way to argue or discuss with those words. That is why I never allowed my boys to answer with those words. Communication is the one great skill that needs to be developed. I have a strong feeling that Marge was rarely asked what do you think or feel. If you are not using those words, you need to start today. It is elemental to the development of your personality and belief system. Remember that just because they are your children they don't have to have the same feelings and ideas that you do. Thank god we all have different opinions about every subject or it would be a boring world.

I read a story recently about a man who is touring the country through the church world teaching parents, mostly fathers, how to write a letter to their children. It is something that has merit I believe. Since the face to face thing seems to be impossible to perform, ANY connection is better than none. I believe that it could be a starting point for future discussions. It might just be like priming the pump. Once it gets started, it may just turn into a river of emotion. If you feel that you are still more distant with any relationship that you'd like to have closer, why not give it a try. The other party involved is dying to hear your words.

Sorry I jumped ahead on the circle, but stay with me and I will connect it for you again. **As your baby feels the safety of your touch and the warmth of your voice, you are laying down the first important brick on the path to the wholeness of love.** It is just not the same with a nanny. The connection of heart and mind has some magical code that is imbedded deep in the DNA strain. It just might be confusing to your child that they spend more time in the arms of someone other than their parents. I believe it has a long term effect that may be difficult to unravel as life goes on.

Remember my equation earlier in the book?

$$\text{Love} = \frac{\textbf{Support} + \textbf{Empathy}}{\text{Time}}$$

If you are focused on work to the point where you lose the value of time spent with your children, don't be surprised when you feel an imbalance at certain points in your life. Time is the key element in the equation and there is NO replacement for it. In hindsight, would you trade it for a bigger house or a nicer car? **I promise you that the only legacy that counts when you are gone is the happiness of your children.** Of that I am certain.

Here comes a sensitive but important issue. Baby talk is fine for about two weeks time. That's right, about two weeks. The formative action of the brain is working like an empty sponge. It soaks up everything it hears because there is nothing else taking up space. Let's not commit a great deal of valuable memory space to baby talk. It won't be used again for long time, when you are giggling in bed with your lover. You know what I mean! That is an approved use for baby talk.

Tone of voice is more important in the early stages of their hearing and learning than actual words. Gentle cooing and touching of the face with your face and hands are highly recommended. You are establishing a safety net of caring so that as words begin being used, the imprint of your voice is already established. Do you see your nanny having the same effect? Sorry nannies of the world…you can take over when the children are in grade school and mom needs to go back to work to re-establish her own self value. You may feel that this time is not important because you are not getting any feedback from your baby. Ignore that thought because it is not about you. That's right; it is not about you at all. It is only about making a nest for your baby to feel safe in. **Just like a momma bird and her baby, you are preparing them for the day when they are going to fly on their own. If you don't help them develop their wings, their first flight is going to have grave consequences.** Damn that is a great analogy! I enjoyed every minute of feathering that nest because I saw the effect it had on me as I grew up at home. There was never a lack of touching or talk at any time in my youth. There was parenting with a purpose every day. Priorities were made very clear by both parents. I still feel that time paying dividends still today. I can see that circle in the eyes of my boys when we get to sit down and talk about things that are important to them. They have NO DOUBT that they can talk about absolutely anything safely with me. There is no such thing as a taboo subject. Would you rather they talked about the serious stuff with someone else or even worse, hold it in and just make poor judgments?

I am about to point to something that people ALWAYS say about my boys and I am not certain exactly where it comes from. The neighbors and friends were always saying how much they enjoyed talking with my children, even when they were just children. I can remember watching Jonathan walking down the street to John and Melinda's house just to sit on the front steps and have a conversation with them. You know, about real stuff, not just silly kid talk. My first instinct is that there was always a very strong emphasis in quality dinner time face to face talk. It appears to be a lost art today. I have heard from many people and friends that they rarely if ever sat down and talked around the dinner table. I believe we have visited this subject earlier in the book and now want to emphasize the VALUE OF TIME SPENT FACE TO FACE AT THE DINNER TABLE! This is where the words, what do you think or feel, start showing up on a regular basis. Opinions are shared by all and opinions are changed and challenged by each other. The secret to all this is that there is no one right answer or opinion. It is amazing the things I have learned from listening closely to what my boys said around the dinner table. I heartily endorse the concept of NO TV during dinner. It is the most valuable time a family can have. I remember once sitting next to a gentleman on a plane that actually made his children do research on a subject and make a presentation at the dinner table. This was a bit over the top for me but also made clear the point that face to face communication skills were honed right there with a purpose. There really is nothing on TV that is of much value to the heart and mind. It is the only thing my mom and dad ever argued about. After a day of work and commuting downtown, my pop liked nothing better than plopping down in his favorite chair and zoning out to the tube. The Honeymooners were his favorite and to this day, my brother Dave knows the words to many of the shows. I believe his sons bought him DVDs of the series for Christmas a few years ago. Yet, until we were in high school and active in all kinds of sports and activities, the dinner table was a shrine of quality family time.

There is a very physical side to communication. Words that are couched in anger or sarcasm have a very cutting edge and scar/wound for a long time. My mother taught me that if you are in doubt, you should hesitate. That holds very true for words. It is very difficult to take back words. I try my best to think things through before saying them for that very reason. In the early stages of my relationship with Colleen she would say things that would hurt my feelings for days. It was because I cared so deeply for her that the hurt was the same depth. We finally figured out that she threw verbal "spears" as a child to simply get attention in a household in chaos and filled with many children. I would tell her what she said and she would say "that's not what I meant." I would repeat her words and say again "that is what you said." It got to the point where she got tired of defending things that she said but didn't mean. So be careful of your attitude when you are speaking because words are so hard to take back.

There is another side of physics and communication that is very important. To our children, we look the size of giants when we tower over them. This can be very intimidating if you can picture any time you have felt out sized by another person. For that reason, in the early stages of your communication with your child, bend or preferably squat right down to their eye level when talking with them. The message you send by doing that will make your words less intimidating and they will hear what you say to a greater degree that if you were towering over them.

Be mindful of your physical layout when you are having discussions with others. If you want to have a chance at more casual conversation, come out from behind your desk and sit across from someone. There is a definite change of power when you are on equal footing. I found that Marge didn't like when we talked in my downstairs office at home, since it felt like "my office" to her. Sometimes it had been necessary for privacy reasons, but if it was later at night, then I would definitely make an effort to find a more neutral space. If that holds true, then sometimes when you want to make sure that your child is listening to your "parent side" and not your "friend side" then your home office may be appropriate for that discussion.

Support + Empathy

It is now time to visit the top part of my love equation, support + empathy. I have been stressing the time function of the equation for some time now. Yes, I firmly believe that the sacrifice of material goods is a valid concept in exchange for more time spent with your child. However, **time spent with your child alone is not a measure of love!**

The secret to making time together with your child valuable is being 100% focused on your connection to your child's interests. If you think that just arranging your schedule to make time to be together is enough, you are mistaken. Support and empathy is the mortar that makes the path hold together. By that I mean that if you are invited to come to grade school for an activity and instead of working directly with the children, you are chatting the entire time with another mom in attendance, you have missed the point. If you come to a soccer game and instead of watching the game you read the paper on the sideline, you have missed the point. If you go for a walk in the woods on a Saturday morning with your child, but spend most of that time with your ear to your cell phone, you have missed the point.

The goal of your time together should be letting your child know that you support their effort unconditionally and are in attendance because you simply love being with them and want to encourage their interests and independence in any way you can. What is important to them should be what is important to you, that is empathy. You are not there to revel in their performance. You can enjoy their performance for their passion and effort, but you support their effort unconditionally. I have seen parents take this time together and twist the child into tears because their effort didn't match the parental expectations. It would be better to not be there if the child feels the pressure to perform at a different level than he or she are capable of.

Often I have heard parents yell comments that make their child feel smaller due to a lack of effort or result. That expectation and presentation have no place in a public, it reflects poor judgment. **The sole goal for your time together at school or sporting events is to simply let your child know they are loved.** Your focused attention on their life's effort should be the result of a cumulative caring that began when you first held your child in your arms. You simply love to spend time with them and listen to their excitement about the day's activities. If you have sat and read the paper at the game or talked with the other moms at school instead of focusing on the activities, you will not be able to participate in the discussion. You will have been a distant observer and your child knows it. **This is a part of building the path that begins very early in your child's life and will be an influence in one way or another for the rest of their life.** Please remember that this time of your lives together comes only once and I guarantee that you will be amazed at how quickly this time flies by!

The emotionally damaged adults I know, and there are way too many, seem to have a consistent theme of pain coursing through their veins. They honestly believe that their parents thought their efforts were NEVER good enough or that they were disappointed in the results of that effort. Low self-esteem comes from impossible demands on your self. High self esteem comes from accepting your own abilities and being proud of your effort, not just a win/loss record. **We parents are not responsible for our child's self esteem in total, yet our guidance and acceptance in these early formative years lays a blueprint for the future**

walks on the path. The opposite behavior establishes a firm foundation for a wall that over time is hard to break down. They simply want our empathy and support of the effort they make in the activities they choose to participate in. Simply put; make an effort as a parent to give less presents and more "presence" in their lives.

The Wall

The opposite of love is not hate, in my eyes, it is indifference. A person can react to hate in a way that can make you stronger as you battle with life for your own growth of self esteem. However, indifference has a debilitating effect that seems to allow your pride and self esteem to slowly leak out of a broken cup. The lack of support by your parents is one of the hardest trials to overcome in a lifetime of inner war for your own self esteem. I have a friend who played football all the way through high school with the sole goal of having his dad say just one positive thing about his effort. Instead, he was typically disappointed to hear about the one tackle he DIDN'T make. He played his heart out and was a team leader although he was not the strongest or biggest of the players. At 45 years of age you might think he would have long forgotten the pain associated with that disappointment. However, this type of lack of support is part of a pattern that usually exists when a parent suffers from their own insecurities and finds it difficult to share or even impossible to share a compliment. This would only lower the parent's own self esteem. **Insecurities like this were typically part of a pattern**

from that parent's own childhood and again are a birthplace of dysfunction. If this chain of insecurity is not broken and empathy is ignored due to a wall of sadness that cannot be breached as it has taken a lifetime to build, you can count on it being part of a family legacy for generations to come.

Lack of real communication due to indifference may be the greatest crippler of children today. The family that NEVER eats together around the dinner table is setting up a recipe for disaster as the year's progress. The lack of communication that comes from parents being too busy or too important to take time for the little ones may be easier to overcome as the child grows up. At least they could see their parent's effort and hopefully reward come to fruition. Once again, it is never too late to make an effort to resurrect the lost time of youth by finding a way to connect to your child's life now. That's what is really funny about life, no matter how old you get, your mom will always be your mom. That spread of time and experience will remain constant as time journeys onward. My mom and I had a wonderful blending of time where our friendship grew larger as I became older. Yet, there were always the times where she reminded me that she was still my mother and as so, had the right to give motherly advice and even ask if I was wearing a heavy enough coat in the winter. I found it endearing that she cared enough to still launch the motherly diatribe regarding my physical well being. She loved being a mother as much as she loved being our friend.

One of my dearest friends is a famous physician in New York. He is a scholar and as well read a person as I know. I find great pleasure in having his company. I also find pleasure in treating him like the average Joe when he is a guest at my house because I can cast a fly rod better than he can and that is a great leveler here in Montana. Anyway, at our wedding recently, he made reference to the time that he was away physically and mentally from his son's early development years. He was thanking me for turning him on to fly fishing all those years ago when we met in Mexico. He brought only spinning gear to a classic salt water destination for fly fishing. I was glad to point him in the right direction on the path to righteousness as a sportsman. That doesn't necessarily mean it comes with casting ability as well. It takes time and effort to master the sport. It is much more difficult than it looks. What I am most grateful for is that the connection to fly fishing has re-established a wonderful link into his son's life over the past ten years. They are now traveling the world together in search of piscatorial splendor. If you can find just one good connection to your child's life that you can become involved in, and then jump at the chance for a re-connection. It wouldn't hurt to even apologize for the time lost in early childhood due to career ambitions. The son has responded with great delight as the dad has taken more time off in order to connect with his son now. The dad has removed the stigma of a son that felt left out as a youth and now has his dad as a best friend. Jim looks happier each time I see them together. His living in the shadow of a famous and renowned father has been replaced by the addition of a great fishing buddy.

I pray for more parents to see the wonder of that familial connection. Frankly, I see it as the tipping point to world peace. If we had less unhappy children in the world I believe

we wouldn't have so many wars and dictators in search of the **power that is making up for a childhood that was devoid of parental love.** I believe that is where bullies in grade school come from. Living in a home of parental indifference may just be hell on earth for a child. There really is no excuse for it. Alcohol and drug problems are typically a result of a child covering up the pain of loneliness that comes from being riddled with fear and doubt as their developmental years passed by without empathy and support of parents.

The physical side of the communication wall begins with that indifference. If your parents do not look you in the eye when they speak to you, there is a reason. Don't look further than the way they were taught to communicate in their childhood. That eye to eye contact is the most important part of a heart felt conversation. If someone is not looking in your eyes when they speak, hold up your hand to stop the conversation and ask them to start over and look in your eyes. It is a great deal harder to lie or be indifferent when looking into someone's eyes. Just try it sometime.

I learned an important lesson early in my parenting life because of this. **I saw early on with my sons that if I was angry and yelled as I was trying to get a message across, then they stopped looking at me out of fear. Once they stopped looking at the sincerity of my anger as I yelled, the message was lost. So, if you want to get your message across, then speak VERY softly.** Have you noticed what happens when someone speaks softly to you? You automatically lean in to hear. If you can control your anger and channel your message in a whispered tone, they will hear you loud and clear because your anger has not stopped their listening.

The same goes for going on too long. The eyes again gave me this hint. One particular time in my office I was trying to make an important message with my son JC. He was paying attention for a while and then I noticed he was starting to glance out the window into the woods behind the house. I asked him what he saw out there that was so interesting. He responded with a quick "nothing." I asked him why he was doing it then and he replied, "You were right about 20 minutes ago, now you are just wearing me out." His answer so surprised me that I almost forgot what I was droning on about. **I learned a very important lesson that day that I have tried to carry on to other parts of my life. Just check yourself the next time you are delivering a message that you want retained. Did you see their eyes glass over or dart away? You probably have gone by the attention reception limit by more than a few minutes.** Give my son the credit for this one as he had the courage to speak up in the face of Mr. Right as he was being lectured. I try not to repeat the same mistakes over and over. It is amazing what we can learn from our children if we listen.

Sarcasm on a regular basis can be a very detrimental tool and creates a wall very quickly. The birth of sarcasm in a relationship may begin between a husband and a wife. Once a pattern of steady sarcasm appears, it may become part of the family's way of communicating. Often followed with the words, "just kidding," words are used as arrows to pierce the heart of a family member. I have seen sarcasm in a very advanced stage and it had progressed to the point where "just kidding" had been eliminated because they usually weren't kidding. See and listen for yourself the next time you say or hear someone say "just kidding." Almost 100 % of the time you will hear those words they will represent an uncomfortable truth that is softened by the kidding words.

The antithesis of sarcasm is sincerity. The trouble is, many people use sarcasm instead of sincerity. It is a major component of the dysfunctional family. The way the sarcasm game is played often leads to an escalation of hurt where adults can act more like children, than children. There is nothing more painful for me than to listen to spouses belittle their mate in front of other people. Often times this happens as a result of feeling safer in the company of others with launching a hurtful comment that has the added bonus of letting other people know how small the spouse wants to make the other feel. Have you seen or felt this? It is painful to watch and has stopped friendship of couples in my life due to the discomfort that this behavior gives off.

The ultimate way for children to grow their self- esteem is to have two parents that treat each other with great respect in front of the children. I can't stress this enough! It is similar to the quality of time issue I just finished describing. If you spend the time with your children belittling your spouse instead of supporting them, then you would almost be better off not speaking at all. I believe that this type of family discord is the source of a great deal of our bullying problem in our schools today. **Kids who are so used to sarcasm and grinding emotional teeth feel no remorse at throwing barbs at other kids as a defense mechanism for their own insecurities.** If you feel that this is a pattern you have fallen into from your upbringing, the time is now to stop the sarcasm! It is as hurtful as hitting someone in the head with a hammer and takes longer to recover from. You can stitch up a flesh wound but it takes forever to heal a childhood filled with painful emotional barbs. Instead, try using these words daily, "have I told you that I love you today?" For some reason in my life there has been a warm aura around those words and it becomes a mantra that the children long to hear. It is a simple confirmation of love that seems to linger in the heart a long while between uses. I have seen other people adopt it after hearing a few times. It has a loving, magical quality to it. So, the next time you are about to launch a bit of sarcasm so that the other person feels smaller, instead try these new words and feel the effect that is creates. If just one person tries it, I win. That is my master plan through all of this. The source of world peace just might be the simple and healthy connection of love within every family. The tipping point of world peace might just be family harmony, one family at a time.

Again the circle connects for me when you analyze the effect that sarcasm has on a lifetime. If you become a user of sarcasm during your childhood, then you are more likely to use it as a tool in your business life as well. You will not be an effective team player because others will resent you for trying to make people in the group feel smaller, so that you can feel bigger. Your own insecurity will be noticeable to your co-workers as you try to fit in with a style that makes your comrades uncomfortable. For me, sincerity goes all the way back to the first page of the first chapter. If you can find the emotional strength to take someone's face in your hands and say, "There is nothing I wouldn't do for you" then it will be near impossible to hurt them with any other emotional barbs. You might even try looking in the mirror and trying it on yourself first, just to feel the impact. If your childhood was filled with sarcasm and hurt, then you may have to forgive your parents for their transgressions. You may even have to work backwards and hold their face in your hands and say the magic words to them. That unconditional love thing can work both ways. Once it is unearthed and used at the right moments, it can become a powerful force in your life. I have seen it change people in a very short period of time. They/we are all very hungry for the confirmation that someone loves us just for being ourselves. **Sincerity is the source of unconditional love. Sarcasm is the source of hurt and painful rejection for a child that will create a wall that the child might hide behind the rest of their life.** The playground is filled with children who are starving for a kind word. Look around the grade schools for those children who find it near impossible to look you in the eye when they speak and I will show you a family that treats each other badly as a recreational way of communicating. Break the chain of this dysfunctional behavior and you will find the teacher's job becoming easier each day.

A teacher can tell in the first week of first grade who is being supported at home and who isn't. I helped edit or type enough of Marge's report cards to hear her sadness at knowing that a child wasn't being supported at home. If your communication skills are lacking due to a childhood deficiency, start as early as you think reasonable with reading on a regular basis to your child. It will at least establish a pattern of communication that is positive. There will be plenty of time for additional efforts at making your child feel the support they so desperately need to become whole. If you wanted to pick just one brick to start your path of safety and love for your child to walk on, pick this one. Sincerity is the mortar that bonds your words together. I guarantee you that sarcasm will create a wall that you will someday be unable to see over if you try to communicate properly with your child. Take a close look at this subject and see if the One Commandment spells out an easy choice here. Forgive your parents if they hurt you, and don't inflict this behavior on your own children. I promise you it will make a great change in your life!

You know, I just decided that this might be the source of the answer I was looking for earlier in this chapter. My boys are great to talk with because of this sincerity thing. They have little time for people who don't understand the merit of heartfelt, direct conversation. The mirror we used to raise them ONLY reflected sincerity and kindness. Even when love was uneven between Marge and me, we rarely if ever, resorted to making the other partner look bad in front of our children. I believe everyone loses when this type of behavior is utilized. I have seen the toll it takes on a heart.

Chapter Nine

Trust

The Path

Trust is the mortar that holds all the bricks together for your path to your child's heart and mind. Trust with your child begins the day you first hold him/her. Your comfort or discomfort is translated directly through your touch. The one word that you need to stay focused on throughout your child's life is safety. If your child feels safe, then they will be able to use all the time they spend at home to develop the personality and feelings that are theirs by nature. If they don't feel safe, then they will build a wall around their heart to protect themselves from harm. It is that simple.

Emotional safety is as important as physical safety during the early development years. Let's consider the One Commandment again. If you remember things that were said or done to you during your childhood that made you feel uncomfortable, write them down and make a special effort to eliminate them from your child's life. I have seen dads who seem to be uncomfortable with the physical intimacy of holding their child. It then extends to playing with them. If that was you and you wish your dad or mom would have gotten on the floor and played with you, then take a deep breath and jump back into your childhood. There is such a short time to enjoy the early years with your children! Before you know it, they will be taking your car. Once that happens, everything changes. Yet, there is a big connection between trust and the day they take your car for the first time by themselves. If you haven't laid a path between you and established a bond of trust, that car moment can be a real tester of a relationship. You need to feel comfortable with where they are going and who they are going to be with. If you have spent time looking in their eyes and talking from the heart, you stand a better chance of knowing when they are telling the truth. **All children will test that trust issue from time to time.** My little angels all had moments of quicksand at their feet when we found out that the truth had not been told. This is an apex of parenting. **How you act when a child betrays that trust carries a great deal of weight. I have found that abject disappointment combined with some liberties taken away is a good combination.** Yelling a great deal has a tendency to lose the message in the madness. My investment in time and sincerity over the years had laid the ground work for these moments. If you haven't spent much time being honest or consistent in your connection with your child, this moment can be a deal breaker.

Don't have high expectations of truth and honesty at these moments if you haven't visited here before.

There is a cumulative effect to this trust issue. You need to establish this pattern of honesty and trust from the day you bring your child home from the hospital. It comes early from your touch and sound of your voice. The gentle pattern of consistency that you use in your tone of voice is the first recognition that your child will have with you. That's one more reason to skip the nanny thing. You need to have that first connection be to your own voices. It is where the true sense of family begins. Your voice and touch are the mortar that will carry your child safely to the point of actual recognition of words and then conversation. Baby talk is good for about a few months. Then you can use the voice that will be the path that they will learn to follow and trust as time goes on.

I have seen fathers in particular that are very uncomfortable with holding their child. This is a common theme that clearly extends back to their childhood and feelings that have carried over to their own parenting effort. Holding and changing the baby is not just a mom job. Fathers, you need to suck up your courage and just sit in a comfortable chair with your precious gift in your arms! Humming your favorite tune or gently talking to your baby will establish a link to the day when you are looking them in the eye as teenagers and hoping you know them well enough when they take off in your car. I believe that is how cumulative this trust issue is with your child. If you haven't hugged your child enough for them to feel safe in your arms, then don't count on them feeling connected enough to tell you the truth about any of their activities. I can tell in a very short time if a man is comfortable with being hugged. I swear it goes all the way back to the childhood path that was never completed. The physical connection that you start that first week at home is the first brick in that path of safety.

I have also seen fathers who know they should be playing with their child and don't have the history of being played with properly as a child. They have a tendency to play a little too rough with their children. They probably had the same treatment as a child and don't know any better way to relate. **Gentleness is just about the manliest trait for a man to develop.** There is something very attractive to women about a man who has the capability to be gentle. Any old caveman is born with the macho thing that most men see as the way to act. However, it takes a special man to be gentle and kind. My father was a champion at this. This is where you start a strong trusting physical relationship with your child. The moment you first have the baby in your arms, realize what an amazing gift you have been given. The way you were treated in the past is just that; the past. I recently came up with a magical sentence that would be good to introduce here. I was talking with someone about the book and why it made sense to share this information. I described the moment where many people say that they just don't think their parents knew what to do with them as they grew up. What we may have taken as dislike, might have been just not knowing any other way. For that reason, I came up with this magical idea. **If you want to be a good parent, you need to visit the One Commandment on a regular basis. The magical beginning of the sentence is, "I** wish my parents would have...." In the business world replace parents with boss and see the same effect. Take any words that come to mind and put them into practice. Again, this is a very simple idea that may help you develop ways to make your parenting more fun and fulfilling as you watch your children grow.

Honesty is also the mortar that makes parenting a great deal more complete. The cumulative effect of consistent truth is that your children will know that they can count on sound advice as they run into issues that confront them. Yes, sometimes that will mean that you tell them what you were like growing up and even some of the things you may not be proud of. Like the empathy part of my equation, it has tremendous value if you can remember to relate your life experiences to your children. I am afraid that as we grow into adults and parents, we often times draw a more strict line in regards to behavior that we had for ourselves. **Consistency in guidelines laid out can be tricky if we don't do as we say and do.** Children are a great deal smarter and aware of things around them than we may give them credit for. So, for example, if you talk to them in harsh tones about drinking and you drink fairly hard on the weekends, don't expect a miracle when they are first confronting the alcohol issue. **Leading by example can be the best or worst way to teach our children, depending on how you are leading.**

One of my songs titled "Watch Over Me" deals with another side of the trust issue. It has to do with explaining the tough side of everyday events and being honest about them. The song points to the first day of school as a time where I needed to make sure that I had someone watching over me as I headed off into the big bad world by myself for the first time. If the issue of separation and where I would find you after school has been dealt with properly in advance, there is going to be a great deal less of kicking and screaming as mom is leaving. I remember very clearly standing at the end of the driveway as my children went off for the first time to school. It was a culmination of many years work to prepare them for that fateful day. Another example is if you tell your child that going to the dentist is fun and they have nothing to worry about, so you can first get them to sit in the chair, then they might not trust you the same way the next time you tell them something. Honesty is the best policy applies to almost everything you can communicate to your child.

It's funny that there are even more serious issues that convene in relation to this subject. The most interesting and controversial subject to me is that of the "DARE" program. I have heard kids say that they thought 5th grade was a bit early to be dealing with the subject of drugs and alcohol. What is more interesting in discussions with teenagers is that they felt that the effort was wasted in one other very important way. There is a great deal of dangerous talk about drugs and alcohol in the program. Then they see their parents drinking or their friends using drugs and they feel like they have been lied to about the dangerous side of use. It makes them believe they can feel safe in trying just about anything because what we told them about drugs and alcohol in the "DARE" program turned out to simply be scare tactics. Instead of "Just Say No" as a policy, I have tried to teach "Just Say Self Respect." At least it is a more honest way to deal with the issue of alcohol and drugs. Most children will experiment with both and we need to make sure they can come to us for honest answers as they run into questions they need to discuss with someone. Why not set up the framework for those days in their early years. What that takes is being honest on a cumulative basis so they know they can count on us. Integrity is something we earn as our children grow older and they decide who they should be asking for serious questions. It is cumulative to their early years in more ways than you can imagine. So when pressed, tell the truth. That way it is easier to remember what you have said.

One of the more difficult trust issues to be consistent with is our attitudes and the way our children perceive them. I still struggle with it all the time. When Colleen says, "What's wrong?" and I say "Nothing" it usually is not nothing. It is usually something and I am either not in the spirit to discuss it or it is something too sensitive or true to be discussed at the moment. I know I do it on a regular basis. If your children pick that mood up from you when you say "nothing" and they can see you are upset, then that message becomes distorted. I am also known as a funny guy around the family. I have always tried to make sure that my children know when I am "just kidding." It got to the point that when I needed to make sure they knew I was serious about a subject, that I actually said out loud, "Do you hear my serious voice?" They were pleased I believe to know when the serious voice was being used that it was time to pay attention and take to heart what I was saying.

Most of this trust issue is definitely a two way street. The main thing you need to accomplish as your children grow older is to simply be aware of who they really are. If you have had consistent contact and conversation in the early years of development, then you will have a better grasp of issues as they grow older. Once that pattern of contact is established as trust, then you will find that you can have a better picture of your child's beliefs and ideas. **Remember, every child will have DIFFERENT ideas and beliefs and staying in touch with each child's feelings will make us a much better resource for dealing with their heart and mind in the future.**

Somewhere along the line we developed a concept of consistent behavior that made a family rule of "We never get angry about accidents." For some reason, I don't know if it started in my childhood or later, I felt there needed to be a clear delineation between accidents and bad behavior. I think it sent a very good message of trust to the boys. They knew if they came to us with a plausible story as to how something happened, then the retribution would be dealt with in a more experienced based consequence. I have seen some parents go off on the kids as if every accident was on purpose. Yelling and screaming at your children for simple mistakes will create a scenario where they will be less willing to take chances in other things that they want to attempt. This applies to many phases of their life. From the first time they make a mistake reading and you don't make fun of them, instead support and help their effort, you will be encouraging experimental behavior. It also makes it easier to discuss things that were clearly not accidental. Bad judgment is one thing and heinous behavior is another. Make the difference black and white and you will have an easier time doling out the punishment and the words to go along with it.

The Wall

The easiest way to destroy trust in any relationship is to not tell the truth. Once that path has been destroyed, you can count on walls being built. Being consistent in your demeanor is a very valuable way to establish trust. Having inconsistent reactions to various situations will make children wary of your behavior and they will not reach out to you. Most of the stories I have heard from my unhappy, adult children, friends are usually based around this area of family. They felt they didn't have anyone in their life they could count on. **Parents wrestling with their own demons are not typically the ones that children feel safe in talking to.**

If you are a struggling parent and it is because of alcohol or drugs, you need to understand that children don't really blame the alcohol or drugs. The child/parent connection began so far back in their history that they see it as one long movie. You only have one chance at trust. Don't think for a minute that it is excusable to abuse your children either physically or emotionally because you were abused. Re-visiting the One Commandment one last time makes that very clear. If you didn't like being abused, then STOP IT TODAY! There are all kinds of resources for you to find help with these days. There is absolutely no reason to punish a child for transgressions against you. You need to break the chain today, not tomorrow.

One of the saddest moments I have seen in people's eyes are the stories about their childhood where the child couldn't even count on being picked up at school. I simply cannot picture a 3rd grade child standing at school and not knowing whether someone was coming to get them or not. Not just on time pick up, but being picked up at all. That is so far from the childhood I had that it staggers me in its cruelty; just how you earn back that trust defies any of my logic. The wall created by that one action, let alone repeated action, must be as high as the moon. You need to be responsible to and for your children. Frankly, it is the most important job you have while here on the planet.

It may be time to go back and read the first page of the book now. If you have come this far in your reading, you have at least been piqued by the subject matter. If you want to keep your child from building a wall around their heart, take their face in your hands, look them in the eyes and tell them "There is nothing I wouldn't do for you!" It is never too late and never too early to say these words to your children. We are ALL hungry to hear them....

The Reward for Building a Path

There is a very real reward for investing the right amount of time and love in your children and all relationships. It is the only way I know to feel the connection to immortality. **By creating or sustaining a chain of kindness, respect and love for your children and fellow man, you will have the faith that your time on this earth was not spent in vain.**

You may not like the truth at times. Here is one truth you can depend on. Five minutes after you die, people will not remember what you had, but will clearly remember who you were and how you treated them.

My greatest reward for building a path to my children's hearts and minds is that I *always* have someone I can count on. As your life evolves, job changes and location changes create periods of time where you might be unsettled. Having a base of family and friends that you know will be there for you can ease those times of uncertainty. Frankly, my three sons are my best friends. I believe I have left the world a better place by simply giving my all to my boys and knowing that they will pass on to their children the gift that my parents gave to me. Is there any greater legacy than that?

More importantly, as I face my own mortality some day I know I will have no regrets. Listening to my friends who have lost the connection to their parents and siblings emphasizes the impact that dysfunction creates. There is a very real hole in the heart of someone who cannot count on their family for support. Often times that hole is filled up with drugs or alcohol to ease the pain of loneliness. If you are in this situation in any way, try reaching out again. The chain can be re-established if just two people care. Let your legacy be one of love, not regret.....

The Trayser Family Prayer

Let us be grateful for the spirit
that holds a family together,
For the infinite beauty of the Earth,

For the opportunity to make
one new friend each day through kindness and
giving without measure,

For if we pass this way but once,
it will be the only legacy we leave....

—John Richard Trayser

About the Author

John Trayser is not a professionally trained counselor or psychologist. He is a father who is hoping to eliminate the increasing number of children and adults in therapy. The gift of unconditional love that his parents gave him has been handed down to his three boys in a way that lets them feel safe every day of their lives.

His success in the business world was based on the ability to build relationships easily by treating EVERYONE like family!

People today are still drawn to his enthusiastic ability to see the best side of everyone he meets.

John lives in the mountains of Montana and pursues his love of fly fishing around the world. He owns the "Bonefish Beach Club" on Andros Island in the Bahamas and is a world class caster. He is a talented musician and songwriter and you can find his CD's at: www.thegreatfuldad.com. His three sons are also musicians and are known to jam on the deck on every occasion possible. He is a partner in Farm2Market Records, a label based in Montana and travels the country promoting the label's artists.

If you need a speaker for an event that requires a positive message, you will find that John has the ability to touch people's hearts with his stories and sincerity in a way that you have not witnessed before. He is Lighthearted not Lightheaded in his daily pursuit of happiness for others...visit greatfuldad.com to contact him for your event.